KNOWING THE TRUTH ABOUT CREATION

Knowing the Truth about Creation

*How It Happened and
What It Means for Us*

Norman L. Geisler

SERVANT BOOKS
Ann Arbor, Michigan

Published by Servant Books
P.O. Box 8617
Ann Arbor, Michigan 48107

Cover design by Steve Eames
Cover illustration by Douglas A. Bowles

Printed in the United States of America
ISBN 0-89283-389-0

89 90 91 92 93 10 9 8 7 6 5 4 3 2 1

Library of Congress Cataloging-in-Publication Data

Geisler, Norman L.
  Knowing the truth about Creation.

  (Knowing the truth)
  Bibliography: p.
  1. Creation. I. Title. II. Series.
BS651.G43 1989   233'.11   88-33627
ISBN 0-89283-389-0

Contents

Publisher's Preface

Servant Books is a publishing outreach of The Sword of the Spirit, an international Christian community whose members represent virtually every stream of church tradition: Protestant, Catholic, and Orthodox. While respecting the differences that divide them, members of The Sword of the Spirit are able to live and serve the Lord together in a united way by focusing on the foundational truths that all faithful Christians hold in common.

Books in the *Knowing the Truth* series aim to express these core realities of the faith in a way that helps all Christians recognize and appreciate the treasures of our shared heritage.

John C. Blattner
Servant Publications

General Editors' Preface

Books in this series have a threefold purpose: to make disciples of Jesus Christ, to lead Christians on to maturity, and to advance the cause of unity within Christ's church. The goal is to convince, edify, and unify by responding to the challenges of unbelief, the cry of spiritual hunger, and the schismatic attitudes of mind and heart that press upon us so hard at the present time.

Our situation is one in which dissent and departure from the essentials of the Christian faith, as revealed in the Bible and set forth in the Creeds, grow steadily worse. The crisis of pluralism escalates, and this bewilders new inquirers, unsettles old saints, disrupts the internal fellowship of churches, and undermines the work of shepherding the flock and evangelizing the world. It is this situation that has called the series into being.

The editors and authors are united in their conviction of the truth and wisdom of the "old paths" of what C.S. Lewis called "mere Christianity"—the ancient orthodox faith on which all Christians fed for the first eighteen centuries. This common belief is no vague, weak "lowest common denominator," but a solid, wide-ranging spread of belief and practice that has been at the heart of every mainstream Christian body from apostolic times.

In many centers of so-called Christian teaching today, clear and definite truth—revealed truth or dogma, to use the time-honored terms—is no longer thought to be available. What formerly went under these names is dismissed as culturally determined fancy, and fresh fancies that are only too obviously spin-offs from modern secular thought are set in their place. This is a tide that we hope our series will help to turn.

The writers' liberty to express their views has not been restricted in any way. Each addresses a readership that includes Roman Catholics, Protestants, and Orthodox Christians, presenting basic truths on which these heritages have at their best been one and commending them as wisdom urgently needed at this time. Each believes and strives to observe the sound old maxim: "In essentials, unity; in nonessentials, liberty; in all things, charity."

These expositions of Bible-based, Christ-centered, Spirit-taught, church-oriented, life-changing Christianity now go out with the prayer that in showing forth the common core of Christianity, they will present clear and cogent testimony to our bemused world, and effectively stabilize and build up the people of God.

J.I. Packer
Peter Kreeft

Introduction

THE TRUTH ABOUT CREATION is not limited to the arena of science. There are also biblical, philosophical, moral, and spiritual dimensions to the topic. In fact, one could argue that the truth about creation is preeminently a spiritual and philosophical matter since creation presupposes a creator, a matter which lies beyond the empirical rigors of science. This book is an attempt to discuss all of these dimensions of creation. Of course, in a work of this length, the treatment cannot be exhaustive but only suggestive.

The aim is not to defend a particular doctrinal point of view but to emphasize what orthodox Christians hold in common. Thus, Part One opens the discussion by turning to the biblical view of God and creation, including both spiritual and material creation. Then, in Part Two, we explore the philosophical and scientific aspects of creation. In Part Three, we turn to the seldom discussed moral and spiritual implications of creation.

Throughout the book, stress is laid on the importance of correctly understanding the doctrine of creation in order to understand God, ourselves, and the whole order of creation. The significance of creation becomes clear as we see its many ramifications in light of the biblical teaching. Creation is said to be the basis of marriage (Mt 19:4-6), the foundation of authority in the church (1 Tm 2:11-14) and in the home (1 Cor 11:3-8, 9), the ground for human government (Gn 9:5-6), and even the basis for ecology (Ps 24:1-4). Furthermore, the reality of creation is integral to the doctrine of original sin and salvation (Rom 5:12, 17), the resurrection of Christ and believers (1 Cor 15:45-49), and the Second Coming of Christ (2 Pt 3:3-11).

The overarching significance of the doctrine of creation cannot be overstated. It is foundational for understanding other important doctrines of the Christian faith. That is why it is not surprising that there are nearly three hundred references to creation in the Bible from Genesis to Revelation.

To aid the reader in the study of creation, I have collected these references to creation into an appendix: Appendix 1, Biblical References to Creation. One can either prayerfully review them over time or pursue a systematic and thorough Bible study of creation.

Moreover, to help guide the reader through the different views held by both Christians and non-Christians on creation, I have organized another appendix (Appendix 2), which lays out the four basic views of creation. My hope is that this appendix will serve as a trustworthy point of reference as readers make their way through *Knowing the Truth about Creation*.

To sum up, in this short survey I have tried to examine the wider significance of the doctrine of creation, not only scientifically but spiritually, not only philosophically but morally. Once all these aspects of creation have been considered, it is my firm belief that the conclusion will become unmistakably clear: without the reality of the Creator, there is no basis for the dignity of man the creature. When the Creator "dies," or is relegated to a mere impersonal first cause, then so does the creature made in his image. In short, the very dignity of man and the meaning of life itself are based on the reality of God as the Creator.

Likewise, our creatureliness explains our fundamental

need to worship and give glory to God. That is, we owe worship to God as our loving Creator who made us to glorify himself and to enjoy him and his creation. Quite simply, that is our final end. And in that light, we are called to an absolute respect for human life, which is made in God's image for his glory. Anything less is tantamount to grave disrespect for God the Creator.

It is my sincere hope that reading this book will not only help to clarify the truth of creation, but also point to the supreme importance of God, the Creator of all. My prayer is that the reader will perceive anew the fundamental nature and the significant implications of this profound doctrine of the faith. By realizing the divine origin of mankind and the cosmos, may each of us better fulfill our God-given obligations to our Creator, our fellow beings, ourselves, and the earth of which we are stewards.

Norman L. Geisler
Lynchburg, Virginia

Part One

What the Bible Tells Us about Creation

ONE

God and Creation

HOW CAN WE KNOW THE TRUTH about creation? For Christians such doctrinal truth is found in God's revelation to man which reveals his purposes.

Therein we discover that God's plan starts and ends with the mystery and the wonder of creation. Creation is the first doctrine to be stated in Scripture (Gn 1:1) and one of the last to be restated (Rv 4:11; 10:6; 21:5; 22:13). The books from Genesis to Revelation contain hundreds of references to creation and the Creator. The word "create" (*bara*)[1] describes three great events in Genesis 1: the creation of matter (vv. 6-10), of living things (vv. 11-12, 20-25), and of human beings (vv. 26-30). All these things that have been created reflect the Creator himself. As such, they show forth his glory. Thus, after each act of creation, Scripture tells us, "And God saw that it was good" (see Gn 1). As the Creator, God was the first to enjoy the wonder and goodness of his creation.

The Universe

"In the beginning God created the heavens and the earth." With these majestic words the Scriptures begin their description of the origin of all things. Creation is the foundation of everything else that follows. This grand statement of the initial divine act is entirely monotheistic. God is one and all-powerful as he creates the earth. Recent discoveries in ancient Ebla (Syria) parallel the Genesis account of creation from nothing (*ex nihilo*). The Ebla creation epic declares:

> Lord of heaven and earth:
> the earth was not, you created it,
> the light of day was not, you created it,
> the morning was not, you created it,
> the morning light you had not [yet] made exist.[2]

The biblical doctrine of creation is centered in the pre-incarnate Christ. He is the *logos* (reason) by whom the *cosmos* (universe) was created. Creation is not only derived *from* God, but it came about *through* Christ. For "all things were created through him" (Col 1:16). In fact, "without him was not anything made that was made" (Jn 1:3). Christ also holds the creation together in his person (Heb 1:3). He is truly the cosmic Christ, by whom all things came to be and in whom all things continue to be.

Statements of Scripture on the origin and nature of the universe teach that creation reflects its Creator while they clearly show the differences between he who is above and beyond what he has made. "God is spirit" (Jn 4:24); as such he is the "invisible God" (I Tm 1:17). Indeed, "no one has ever seen God" (Jn 1:18; cf. 1 Tm 6:16). Moreover, as spirit he is incorporeal; he has no "flesh and bones" (Lk 24:39). However, the universe that God created is both visible and material (Heb 11:3). It can be seen and handled, being both physical and tangible. It has both space (whereness) and time (whenness). It possesses both a "here" and a "now." Further, it has matter which is extended throughout space and time to countless galaxies. It has small "parts" or particles with spaces between them.

The matter or "stuff" of the universe is described by modern science in terms of atoms that consist of charged particles of physical energy. In human experience, matter is sensible, tangible, and visible. It is the hard, objective data that comprises our environment—the very stuff we eat, breathe, touch and see as earthbound creatures. We must make our way around it or else knock our head on it. Bodies are real. The earth is tangible, as are the myriads of stars and the planets in our own galaxy, to say nothing of the entire universe.

All of this was created by God in the beginning. "For by him all things were made" (Jn 1:3). God "created all things, visible and invisible" (Col 1:16). He created the "heavens and earth." His creation includes the land, the water, and all plants and animals (Gn 1:1-26). It includes also the human body that was "made from the dust of the ground" (Gn 2:7). There is a real material universe, and it was created by God.

God not only formed the universe, he brought all of matter into existence out of absolutely nothing. As John the apostle proclaimed of God, "Thou didst create all things, and by thy will they existed and were created" (Rv 4:11). The Bible says God simply spoke (Gn 1:1) and things came into existence by his power and word (Heb 1:3; cf. 2 Cor 4:6). "By the word of the Lord were the heavens made, . . . For he spoke and it came to be" (Ps 33:6, 9). The writer of Hebrews declares, "By faith we understand that the world was created by the word of God, so that what is seen was made out of things which do not appear" (11:3). This great God of might and power spoke and creation came forth. Moreover, God's creative Word is Christ himself. "He is before all things," and "all things were created through him" (Col 1:16-17). It was through him that "all things were made," and "without him was not anything made that was made" (Jn 1:3). That is, it was all created out of nothing. As the Word, Christ is the agency of this overwhelming creative power.

This beautiful material universe was created by God but not out of God. The cosmos is not made out of God-stuff. This is why it is a grievous sin to worship and serve the "creature rather than the Creator" (Rom 1:25). It is for this reason that idolatry is condemned so strongly in the Scriptures. God commanded: "You shall not make for yourself a graven image or any likeness of anything that is in heaven above, or that is in the earth beneath" (Ex 20:4). If, on the other hand, the universe were God's "body" or part of his substance, there would be no reason not to worship it. But the Bible makes it very clear that God is not to be identified with the physical universe. The universe comes from God but it is not made of God. God is as different from the world as a potter from clay (Rom 9:20) or as the craftsman is from his handicraft (Ps 19:1). God is totally other.

The material universe is not made out of God, but it is a declaration of God. "Ever since the creation of the world his invisible nature, namely, his eternal power and deity, has been clearly perceived in the things that have been made" (Rom 1:20). We see that God is present in creation both as its sustaining cause (Heb 1:3; Col 1:17) and as it reflects his attributes (Rom 1:20). Just as the creative mind of Shakespeare or Picasso is revealed in his works, so the Creator of the universe can be seen in his great masterpiece.

His grand design is all around us, a feast for the mind and the soul.

The Universe and Its Creator

God is the invisible Creator of the visible world, the immaterial maker of all matter, and the incorporeal producer of all corporeal (bodily) things. How can God create matter when he is not material? In response to this question several points are worth making.

First, it is no greater mystery for the theist to believe that mind produced matter than it is for the atheist who believes matter produced mind. In fact, it is easier to believe that infinite mind can make matter than it is that finite matter can produce a mind that can contemplate the infinite.

Second, it is no more difficult to understand how an immaterial spirit (God) can be manifest in material things than it is to comprehend how our minds can reveal themselves in material things, such as literature, art, and technology. Just as the written page is a material manifestation of the immaterial thoughts of the author, the universe is a material creation of the immaterial Creator. We see the sign of his craftsmanship in the way he has made us.

Finally, in spite of its similarity to the Creator (Rom 1:19-20), creation by its very nature must also be different from the Creator. For God is infinite and creation is finite. He is necessary (independent), and creation is contingent (dependent). God is uncreated, but the world is created. After all, a painting is visible but the artist's mind that created it is not. By its very finite nature creation must differ from its infinite Creator. All creation, whether visible or invisible, partakes of certain characteristics. For instance, every created thing is necessarily finite or limited in scope.

And it cannot create something out of nothing the way God can. Rather the creature, according to its nature and abilities, must act upon something in order to make or form anything. And since the physical universe is part of creation, it also participates in these properties. Like a painter, the Creator gave form and substance to his ideas. And therefore, the creation reflects something of the Creator and shows forth his purpose. We see his mind in it.

The recent discoveries in astronomy of thousands of distant galaxies, for example, reveal something of the sheer magnitude and scope of creation in a particularly arresting way. Astronomer and layman alike are overwhelmed as they consider anew the enormous dimensions of the universe. Yet all of creation is but a reflection of God's own grandeur and glory as the Creator. Not only that, the fact that we as men and women can appreciate the magnitude of the universe demonstrates to us part of God's purpose in creating it and endowing it with grandeur: it is there, in part, for our own enjoyment! In a very real sense, it is God's gift to us!

1. Creation Is Dependent. The created world, including matter, is dependent upon God. Even though the world exists, it could nevertheless not have existed. It is, but it might not have been. Indeed, God is holding it in existence "by his word of power" (Heb 1:3). For by him "all things hold together" (Col 1:17). Without God's continual, sustaining causality, all of creation would cease to be—instantly.

The dependence of all creation is another way to express the biblical truth that God is not only the originating cause of the universe, but he is also its conserving cause. God caused it to come to be, and he also causes it to continue to be. The following chart expresses the two kinds of causality.

God's Causality	
Originating Causality	*Conserving Causality*
Cause of beginning	Cause of sustaining
Cause of coming to be	Cause of being
Cause of coming together	Cause of holding together
Cause of origin	Cause of operation

Creation is dependent at all times. It always relies on its Creator for its existence. Once a creature, always a creature: the created can never become the uncreated. Radical dependence on God for moment-by-moment existence is an essential characteristic of all created things, including the material universe as a whole. You and I, and all created things, would simply cease to be without the Creator and sustainer of all.

2. Creation Is Finite. Another essential property of creation is that it is finite or limited. Only God is infinite or unlimited. It is impossible to have two infinite beings. For infinity includes all, and there cannot be two alls. God is infinite; he includes all perfections. All exists relative to him. As Paul declared, "In him [the Infinite God] we live and move and have our being" (Acts 17:28). When he created finite beings there was not more being; there were simply more who had it, just as when the teacher teaches the class there is not more knowledge; there are simply more who know.

Further, if there were two infinite beings they would have to differ. But they cannot differ by what they do not have. For since each is an infinite being, there is nothing essential to beings each does not have. Neither can they differ by what they do have, since being infinite they both have everything proper to infinite perfection. To differ by nothing is not to differ at all; they are identical. Thus there can only be one infinite being. If there is only one infinite being (God), then all other things—the whole of creation—must be finite. God alone is unlimited; everything else is limited. He is the unlimited limiter of all limited things. He is the uncaused cause of all that is caused.[3]

The very fact that all created things are caused to exist reveals that they must be limited. For if they came to be, then they did not always exist. Hence, their existence is not unlimited; they had a beginning. Furthermore, whatever is created undergoes change. Only God is unchanging. "I, the Lord, do not change" (Mal 3:6). Of the heavens the Scriptures declare:

> They will perish, but thou remainest; they will all grow old like a garment, like a mantle thou wilt roll them up, and they will be changed. But thou art the same, and thy years will never end. (Heb 1:11-12)

Whatever changes is limited, for if it changes then it does not remain exactly what it was. It is limited by what it can become. It cannot be precisely what it once was for in that case it has not changed. Therefore, all changing things are limited.

The fact that created things change reveals that they have the possibility of change. The actuality of change shows the potentiality for change. Thus all created things have potentiality. They *can* change. But all created things also have actuality, since they actually exist. So all created things have both actuality and potentiality. God, on the other hand, is pure actuality. God is the "I AM" (Ex 3:14). He said, "I AM WHO AM." He is what he is. In God there is pure actuality with no limiting potentiality. There is nothing he can be that he has not always been nor always will be. A creature, however, has the potential to be what it is not. Its being is by definition limited. Thus, creatures are limited by their potential.

3. Material Creation Is Spatial and Temporal. In addition to being dependent and limited, material creation is also restricted to space and time. Time is a measurement based on change. It measures "before" and "after" a given change. Because he is an unchanging being, God is not subject to such measurements. Since he is always the same, he cannot be the object of calculations based on what he once was. Because he has not changed, he still is what he always was. However, in changing beings, such as material things are, measurements can be made by comparing their state before and after the change. Time is such a measurement.

Time measures certain limited segments.[4] Temporal beings—that is, those that are in time—are limited to a "now" as opposed to a "then." We never live a then, only a now. We are not now living the past: we lived the past *then*. But the present we are living *now*. Every future moment becomes a "now" when we experience it. We cannot live both a "now" and a "then" simultaneously in the same sense. We can live the past only in memory but not in actuality. Time is a measurement based on a real limitation that we have as material (bodily) and mental (psychological) beings: we are really limited to the "now" we live.

Likewise, space is a limitation. Time is a limitation to a "now," and space is a limitation to a "here." The limitations of space impose upon us the boundary conditions of "hereness" rather than "thereness." We cannot be both here and there at the same time and in the same sense. We can be there mentally (by day dreaming), but we can only be here bodily. As spatiotemporal beings, we are limited to the "here" and "now"; so are all material things. Such is the spatial limitation placed on all material things.

God, however, can be here, there, and everywhere at the same time. For he has no body or any other kind of finitude that limits him to being only here as opposed to there. God has no "hereness" that limits him to one place at a time. God is omnipresent, that is, present everywhere in all of creation at the same time. This is possible because he is an infinite spirit. Having no body to limit him, nor finite capacity to fence him in, God's presence is barred from nowhere. As the psalmist said, "Whither shall I go from thy Spirit? Or whither shall I flee from thy presence? If I ascend to heaven, thou art there! If I make my bed in Sheol, thou art there!" (Ps 139:7-8). Once again, then, we see that God is totally other. He is without limits, unlike us.

4. All Creation Is Good. After nearly every day of creation "God said, 'It is good'" (Gn 1:4, 10, 12, 18, 21). After the final day "God saw everything that he had made, and behold it was very good" (1:31). Indeed, the apostle Paul declared, "Everything created by God is good" (1 Tm 4:4). In the Epistle to the Romans he added, "I know and am persuaded in the Lord Jesus that nothing is unclean in itself" (14:14). Everything God made is good. Like its Creator, all of creation was and still is good.

This Judeo-Christian teaching that material and bodily

things are good stands in contrast to other religions and
philosophies. Gnostics, heretics in the early Christian era,
believed that matter was evil. The third-century pagan
philosopher Plotinus held that it was nearly evil, the least
good of all things. For him it had no good but only the mere
capacity for good.[5] Plato thought matter was a formless
chaos, and identified the good with form. Indeed, the more
radical Eastern belief (e.g., Shankara Hinduism) holds that
matter is an illusion (*maya*). Christian Science believes
matter is evil, an error of mortal mind.[6] But the Bible
declares, "Everything God created is good."

The Unity, Diversity, and Stability of All Life

God not only created matter (Gn 1:1), but he also created
"every living creature that moves" (1:21). All of life exists
because he wills it to exist. The biblical description of life
includes its unity, its great diversity, and its stability, all of
which reflect its creation by God. It has one source but many
manifestations, and continually reproduces itself after its
kind.

1. The Unity of All Life. There are many indications in
Scripture of the unity of all living things. First, all life has
one Creator. His stamp is upon all things. That is why
creation reflects the glory of God. Second, all life is
interdependent. Higher forms were commanded to eat
lower forms (Gn 1:29-30; 9:3). Third, humans were commanded to care for the environment (1:28), to cultivate the
flora and to care for the fauna (2:15). These, in turn, would
provide food and clothes for humans (3:21). Finally, the
Bible often refers to "all living things" as a group or as a
whole (Gn 1:21; 6:7; Acts 17:24). All life comes from one

God; it manifests one creative mind. Each individual form fits into one organic whole.

2. The Diversity of All Life. God loves variety. He created all kinds of things. Genesis 1 describes vividly the forms of life that filled the earth and teemed in the sea. The landscape crawled with animals, the sea swarmed with fish, and birds flew across the heavens. The great diversity and abundance of life reflects, in the biblical view, the bounty of its Creator. In fact, each act of creating was an act of differentiating and diversifying that shows the complimentary nature of the created order in contrast to the uniformism and sameness emphasized in modern society, particularly in the area of sexuality with the blurring of the differences between the sexes. Many great hymns, poems, and prose works have been written about the incredible variety of creation.

3. The Stability of All Life. God provided for the continuance of the life he created. Each was to produce "according to its kind" (Gn 1:11). Thus "plants yielding seed and fruit trees" were made "bearing fruit in which is their seed." The same was true of animals of the sea and land, each reproducing "according to its kind" (vv. 21, 25). Finally, mankind was told to reproduce their kind (v. 28; cf. 5:3). Thus God provided for the ongoing life of each kind he had made. Life is basically the same from generation to generation, each reproducing its own kind: fish spawning fish, birds hatching birds, cows calfing calves, and humans giving birth to human babies. This has been the pattern from the very beginning and continues to the present. Life in all of its many kinds is continuous and stable. Not only, then, does life teem with great variety, it is also sustained by a fine balance.

Human Beings

Mankind is the crown of God's earthly creation. Although humans were "created a little lower than the angels" (Heb 2:7), nonetheless they are higher than the animals. They were made, male and female, in "God's image and likeness" (Gn 1:27).

In the words of Scripture, the "Lord God formed the man of dust from the ground and breathed into his nostrils the breath of life, and man became a living being" (Gn 2:7). Then God "took one of his ribs and closed up its place with flesh; and the rib which the Lord God had taken from the man he made into a woman" (vv. 21-22). Jesus referred to this event, declaring, "that at the beginning the Creator 'made them male and female'" (Mt 19:5). Indeed, Jesus said that the creation of man and woman was the basis for lifelong marriage between husband and wife (v. 6).

The Scriptures everywhere assume that there was first one man and one woman from whom all human beings are descended. Speaking of original sin, the Scriptures refer to Adam as a historical person, just as Moses was (Rom 5:14). Paul also refers to the first man in 1 Corinthians 15 when comparing Adam to Christ (v. 22). Luke places Adam as the first name in the literal, actual ancestry of Christ (Lk 3:38). He adds significantly that Adam is the "son of God." The historical record in 1 Chronicles names Adam as the first human being as well (1 Chr 1:1). Everywhere Scripture assumes or declares that the origin of mankind is the creation of Adam and then Eve, as recorded in Genesis 1 and 2. God created them (Gn 1:27), forming the man from "the dust of the ground" (2:7) and shaping the woman from Adam's rib (v. 21).

What of this first man and first woman that God created? What is their nature as a race? The nature of human beings includes their dignity, their unity of soul and body, and their community as a group of individuals. All human beings came from a common source, and all possess a common human nature. As Paul declared, "He made from one every nation of men" (Acts 17:26).

1. Human Dignity. Mankind is a special creation of God, uniquely made in God's "image and likeness" (Gn 1:27). This is said of no other creatures. Only humans are made in the image of God. This image includes both "male and female." It extends to Adam's children. Even after the fall "Adam . . . had a son in his own likeness, after his own image" (Gn 5:3).

Human life is therefore sacred. Killing or cursing a man or woman is an attack upon God in whose image they are made. The Bible teaches that it is wrong to murder any human being, for "whoever sheds the blood of man, by man shall his blood be shed; for God made man in his own image" (Gn 9:6). James adds that it is even wrong to curse other persons because they "have been made in God's likeness" (Jas 3:9).

This image of God includes both moral and intellectual characteristics. Although humans are finite, nevertheless, they are like God in that they have intelligence. Paul speaks of human nature being "renewed in knowledge after the image of its Creator" (Col 3:10). Since humans were created like God, it is expected that they would share moral characteristics with God as well. Hence, God commands us, "You, therefore, must be perfect, as your heavenly Father is perfect" (Mt 5:48). The Lord said to Israel, "Be holy, for I am holy" (Lv 11:45).

Not only do humans resemble God, but they are to represent him as well. Human beings are to reign as God's agents or stewards on earth. God said to Adam and Eve, "Fill the earth, and subdue it. Have dominion over the fish of the sea and over the birds of the air and over every living thing that moves upon the earth" (Gn 1:28). Man was to be king over all the earth; he was created "little less than God," crowned "with glory and honor" (Ps 8:5). This is truly a holy and serious vocation that God has given to every human being in his or her particular sphere of activity and responsibility. It is nothing to treat lightly.

Moral responsibility implies the ability to respond, both by our own will and by God's grace. Essential to morality is voluntariness: the ability humans have to use their will to choose. Like God, humans have free choice. Indeed, God gave Adam a choice (Gn 2:16-17) and held him accountable for it. Likewise, all who have sinned since Adam are held accountable for their sins (Ez 18:20; Rom 5:14). This ability to choose by using his will gives man a special place over the rest of creation and a special responsibility for maintaining the order of creation.

2. Human Unity. Man's ability to choose is in itself an extraordinary gift. And so, too, the wonder of man's creation is that each individual human being is a unity of soul and body. Each human being has a spiritual dimension and a physical dimension. Each partakes of the immaterial as well as the material, the angelic as well as the animal. Each is a psychosomatic unity, a blend of mind and matter. This makes man altogether unique in creation.

The unity of body and soul is evident from the very beginning. For "the Lord God formed man of dust from the ground [body], and breathed into his nostrils the breath of life [spirit]; and man became a living being" (Gn 2:7). At death "the dust returns to the earth as it was, and the spirit returns to God who gave it" (Eccl 12:7).

Soul and body are so closely united in human beings that their union is used as a figure of what is virtually inseparable (Heb 4:12). Paul speaks of "spirit, soul, and body" forming an individual "wholly" (1 Thes 5:23). He means that they constitute one person. A human being is self-conscious, world-conscious, and God-conscious. He is a tri-unity that can look inward, outward, and upward. He is, nonetheless, one person with one individual human nature.[7]

Within the unity of human nature, there is also a basic duality. The unity of soul and body is not an identity of the two. The union is not an indissoluble one. For at death "we are away from the body at home with the Lord" (2 Cor 5:8). Indeed, such is stated of the blessed whose bodies are "slain" but whose "souls" are conscious in heaven (Rv 6:9).

However, this separation of soul and body is only temporary. We will be reunited with our physical bodies at the resurrection of the dead. The soul and the resurrection body will be brought back together permanently (1 Cor 15:51-55). It is important to see, then, that the intermediate state between death and resurrection is both temporary and incomplete. Paul describes this temporary state as being "unclothed" (2 Cor 5:1-4). After death, we await the return to our natural union of body and soul in a reunion of physical and spiritual dimensions.

3. Human Community. Yet we do not exist simply as separate and unique human beings. We need each other. "No man is an island." From the very beginning God made a community, a family, of "male and female" and told them to multiply into a larger community (Gn 1:27-28). Indeed, before Eve was made, Adam discovered that "it is not good for the man to be alone" (Gn 2:18). The solidarity of all humanity is a fact not only of their original creation but also of their continued existence. Paul declared this when he said that God "made from one every nation of men to live on all the face of the earth" (Acts 17:26). Not only are all human beings one in Adam's creation, but we were also one in Adam's fall. For "sin came into the world through one man . . . so death spread to all men because all men sinned" (Rom 5:12). That is, the whole human race was present in Adam when he sinned, so it fell with him. We all share the same basic life, physically and spiritually.

The unity of the human race is also evident in the means of its propagation, as well as the provision of salvation (Rom 5:12-19). New human beings come only from a union of male and female. From this union children are produced in the "likeness" of their parents (Gn 5:3). The whole race is genetically connected. Indeed, there are many ethnic groups but only one race—the human race. We all have only one father (Adam) and one mother (Eve), who is called "mother of all the living" (Gn 3:20). Hence, we are all part of one large "family" (Eph 3:15).

No one is completely independent. For woman was created from man and yet "man is born of woman" (1 Cor 11:12). There are no self-made men: every man since Adam had a mother. The whole human race is interdependent. We are a community of beings with a common Creator and a common connection.

4. Headship and Submission to Form a Unity. For this human community to remain united in mind, heart, and purpose, God established headship and submission—an order that reflects the very life of God in the Trinity.

In the creation account, God clearly establishes man as the head and woman as his helpmate (Gn 2:18-25) in the garden. In fact, Eve is fashioned out of one of Adam's ribs and is then given to him by God. As head of the human race, the man is addressed first by God after the fall (Gn 3:9); and Christian tradition has always held that Adam's sin is decisive for the fall of mankind.

This fundamental order of headship and submission is reflected in the very life of God himself by the perfect subordination of the Son to the Father in the economy of salvation (Phil 2:5-11). It is not an issue of equality; the three persons of the Godhead share the same divine nature. It is a matter of their respective roles: God the Father is the Creator; the Son is the Redeemer; the Holy Spirit is the Paraclete and Comforter. Therefore, it is not at all surprising that the ordering of relationships in the human community reflects this divine ordering of roles in the Trinity for the unity and common good of all.

In fact, God's plan of creation for the right ordering of human relationships is not only the basis of headship in marriage and family life, but of authority in the church (1 Tm 2:11-14) and in human governments (Gn 9:5-6) as well. Once again, the question is not one of equality but of complementary roles to achieve a unity and to protect the common good.

United in heart and mind and spirit, what exactly is the purpose or common commission of mankind?

The Purpose of Mankind

The purpose of man the creature is twofold: to honor the Creator and to enjoy his creation. This design is evident from the very beginning of creation and from the very nature of the creature.

1. To Glorify the Creator. The purpose of the creature is to glorify his Creator. God said, "I created for my glory" (Is 43:7). This purpose follows from the nature of the Creator as well as of the creature.

Creation did not come by compulsion. The Scriptures say plainly, "By thy [God's] will they existed and were created" (Rv 4:11). God did not need to create. An infinite, perfect being needs nothing. God was not lonely. As a Trinity of persons—Father, Son, and Holy Spirit—God had absolutely perfect fellowship within himself. He did not have to seek any companionship elsewhere. He created only because he wanted to. Our existence is not necessary; we exist only because he wants us to be. Our very nature as freely created beings demands our allegiance to our Creator, who has given us the gift of freedom so we can enter into a filial relationship with him as sons and daughters. To him we owe an immeasurable debt of gratitude for making us and giving us such a destiny.

Not only did we come to be because of God's will, but we also continue to be by his will, for "in him all things hold together" (Col 1:17). If God were to decide that we not exist we would go into oblivion at that very instant. God sustains all things in existence, including mankind. God has given ample evidence of his sustenance of all creation. Without the air he provides and the food he gives, we could not live. It behooves us, therefore, not to bite the hand that feeds us. Rather, as thankful creatures we should join with the psalmist in proclaiming, "At the works of thy hands I sing for joy" (Ps 92:4). As grateful creatures we should glorify "the Creator, who is blessed forever. Amen" (Rom 1:25). This is the very purpose for our existence.

2. To Enjoy God's Creation. God is not a cosmic killjoy or a heavenly scrooge. He desires his creatures to be content.

The psalmist said the Lord "satisfies you with good as long as you live" (Ps 103:5). Paul speaks of "God, who richly furnishes us with everything to enjoy" (1 Tm 6:17).

. God desires his creatures to be happy as well as holy. He wants to provide them with satisfaction as well as sanctification. It is his very purpose that we enjoy every gift he graciously gives. For "there is nothing better for a man than that he should eat and drink, and find enjoyment in his toil. This also, I saw, is from the hand of God; for apart from him who can eat or who can have enjoyment?" (Eccl 2:24).

To sum up, Scripture teaches that God created the physical universe and every living thing. He created human beings in his own image and likeness. Everything was created out of nothing. Material creation by its very nature is dependent, finite, and limited in space and time. It is also good. God created life in all its diversity and gave it an enduring unity and stability to reproduce after its kind. Human beings are a distinct and unique creation, possessing dignity, unity, and community in right order for the common good. Our purpose is to glorify God and to enjoy his creation.

TWO

Material Creation: Man and the Cosmos

WHAT DOES THE BIBLE TEACH US about the physical universe? First, we learn that creation is utterly dependent on God, both for its coming to be and for its continuing to be. The reality of this dependence applies to creation's present status as well as to its past beginning. The universe and everything in it began as God's creation, and it continues to be God's creation. The Scriptures are explicit on this point.

The Hebrew word for "creation" (*bara*) and its Greek counterpart (*ktisis*) are usually reserved for the original acts of creation in the past. That is, they are used to indicate the origin or beginning of things. Creation, properly speaking, is an event that happens once, not an ongoing process. However, God's role as Creator did not stop with the beginning of the universe, and biblical usage reflects this fact as well. For even though God has completed his work *of* creation; nevertheless, he is not finished with his work *in* creation. We see, then, that there is a difference between God's work in the *origin* of the world and his work in the *operation* or continuation of it.

Creation as the Beginning in the Old Testament

Genesis 1:1 (cf. 1:21, 27) speaks of creation as a past event. "In the beginning God created the heavens and the earth." In this passage *bara* [created] obviously refers not to the present functioning of the universe but to its past genesis.

Genesis 2:3 also refers to the acts of creation by which the world began: "God blessed the seventh day and hallowed it, because on it God rested from all his work which he had done in creation." That God rested and is still in that rest demonstrates that the word "creation" is used here in the sense of a series of singular, unrepeated events. Likewise, the next verse (Gn 2:4) places the creation event in the past when it declares, "These are the generations of the heavens and the earth when they were created."

Genesis 5:1 and 2 refer to Adam's and Eve's creation as a past event "when God created man." We read that "Male and female he created them, and blessed them and named them Man when they were created."

In Genesis 6:7 God spoke to Noah, crying out, "I will blot out man whom I have created from the face of the ground. . . ." Even though the reference here seems to be to the whole human race alive in Noah's time, nonetheless, their creation as a race in Adam is referred to by Paul as a past event (Rom 5:12). Of course, God is active in the propagation of the race from this point of beginning (Gn 1:28; 4:1, 25). But the creation of Adam was a past event that has not been repeated since.

Most other occurrences of *bara* in the Old Testament clearly refer to the past. In Psalm 89:11 and 12 the word creation is used to refer to the origin of heaven and earth.

The psalmist declared:

> "The heavens are thine, the earth also is thine; the world and all that is in it, thou hast founded them. The north and the south, thou hast created them." (Ps 89:11-12)

Isaiah 40:26 says God "created" the stars as well as numbered and named them. In 42:5 he also declares that God "created the heavens... [and] the earth and what comes from it." He also "made the earth and created man upon it" (Is 45:12).

Malachi 2:10 also refers to the creation of the human race, saying, "Has not one God created us?" While the race has been propagated since Adam, the Bible makes it clear that it was created in Adam (Gn 1:27; cf. Rom 5:12). So the creation of mankind is viewed as a definite event that is now past. Even Jesus referred to it as an event which occurred at "the beginning [when] God made them male and female" (Mt 19:4).

Creation as the Beginning in the New Testament

Like the Old Testament, the New Testament consistently uses the word creation (*ktisis*) as a past event, not as a present process. In Mark 10:6, Jesus teaches that "from the beginning of creation, 'God made them male and female.'" This leaves no doubt that he is referring to an act of creation as a past unrepeated singularity. He is not describing a regular process observable in the present.

Mark 13:19 employs the word "creation" in the same way, saying, "In those days there will be such tribulation as has not been from the beginning of the creation which God created until now." This is an unmistakable reference to creation as the point of beginning, not a process that is continuing.

In Romans 1:20 Paul declared that "ever since the creation of the world . . . his [God's] eternal power and deity has been clearly perceived in the things that have been made." Paul here is clearly emphasizing in his use of the word "creation" God's original work of making the world.

1 Timothy 4:3 declares that "God created [all foods] to be received with thanksgiving." While foods are being pro- duced in the present, the reference here is to the original creation of food. This is evident from the use of the aorist tense, which indicates a completed action. Also the phrase "to be received" points to the original purpose of the creation of food. We and all creatures are meant to receive our food from God with thanksgiving.

The Book of Revelation uniformly refers to creation as the past work of God by which all things began. John the Beloved Disciple noted Christ's preeminence from the very "beginning of God's creation" (Rv 3:14). The heavenly host around God's throne praise God because by him all things "were created" (4:11). And the angel swears by him "who created heaven and what is in it, . . . and the sea and what is in it" (10:6; cf. 14:7).

In the vast majority of these references there is no doubt that the word "creation" refers to the beginning of the universe (including life matter and mankind), not to its continuance since then. Where a process may be implied, on the other hand, is not in the creation of the physical universe but in the propagation of animal and human life. While the word "creation" is sometimes used in other contexts than the origin of the universe and living things (e.g., Is 45:7), the word chiefly refers to the original, unrepeated, events of creation by which God brought matter, living things, and human beings into existence.

God Continues to Rule over His Creation

Once the world was created, God did not cease to relate to it. In fact, he continually acts in it. His providential presence is manifest in all of his creation. Through Christ he even sustains its very existence (Heb 1:3). Rarely, however, does the Bible refer to God's work at present in sustaining the world as "creation." But there are a few exceptions.

Psalm 104:30 declares, "When thou sendest forth thy Spirit, they are created; and thou renewest the face of the ground." Here the word "create" (*bara*) is used, not to mean the initial generation of life on earth, but the continual regeneration of it. The context speaks of God causing "the grass to grow for cattle, and plants for man to cultivate" (v. 14). He is a God who "makest springs gush forth in the valleys" (v. 10) and who "makest darkness, and it is night" (v. 20). He is a God who continually provides food for all living things (v. 28). In short, the repeated emphasis of the passage is on God's continual operation and preservation of his world. The word "creation" is used to describe this continual activity of God.

Amos 4:13 says that God "creates the wind, and . . . makes the morning darkness." Here too it seems that the word "creation" is used to describe God's work in his creation, not simply his original work of creation. And, in point of fact, the word "make," which is often used interchangeably with the word "create" (cf. Gn 1:26, 27; 2:18), is used on many occasions to describe God's continual work in the world (cf. Ps 104:3, 4, 10).

There are numerous ways the Bible presents God as

presently at work in his creation. He is "making," "doing," or "causing" the laws of nature to operate in various ways. He sustains his creation (Heb 1:3), holds it together (Col 1:17), causes it to have being (Rv 4:11), and produces life in it (Ps 104:14). In short, God is not only the originator but also the operator or sustainer of his world. He is not simply the original cause but the continual cause of its existence. He is Creator and preserver. There would be no reality of creation, past or present, were it not for God. It all utterly depends on him.

God's dual work of creating and preserving the world are often presented in the same passage, even in the same verse. Notice the following contrasts revealing both aspects of God's work. For example, Genesis 1:1 says, "God created the . . . earth." Then later he is at work through the land "producing vegetation" (v. 11). The first was an act of origin; the second was one of operation. Both are acts of God. Genesis 2:3 declares that "God rested" from his original "work of creating." But Jesus affirmed that God "is still working" (Jn 5:17). The former describes the commencement of his work of creation; the latter depicts the continuance of his work in creation.

The New Testament likewise shows God in the same dual role. In Acts 17:24 Paul proclaims that God "made the world." A couple of verses later he says, "In him we live and move and have our being" (v. 28). God is both the past cause of its becoming and also the present cause of its being. Colossians 1:16 expresses God's past work as one by which "all things were created." The very next verse explains, "In him all things hold together." The former is an act of causing it to come to be; the latter is God's act of causing it to continue to be. Hebrews 1:2 declares, "But in these last days he has spoken to us by a Son, whom he appointed the heir of all things, through whom he also created the world." Yet in the very next verse it reveals that Christ is also "upholding the universe by his word of power." Here again one verse refers to Christ creating the world and the other to his preserving it.

The reality of creation is not limited to a discussion of its past beginning but also includes its present continuance. The Creator, as both producer and preserver, is necessary not only to make it but also to sustain it. No picture of creation is complete that neglects God's role in both areas. And no view of creation is complete that fails to see that all members of the triune Godhead are active in creation: Father (1 Cor 8:6), Son (Jn 1:3; Col 1:16, 17; Heb 1:2, 3), and Holy Spirit (Gn 1:2).

Primary and Secondary Causes

Since God's acts are necessary both for the world coming to be as well as for it continuing to be, God is both the commencing as well as the conserving cause of all that exists. Focusing on God as actor, rather than on his actions, reveals two distinctly different roles of God in relation to his creation. In one role he is the originator of it; and in the other he is the chief operator of it. He is both the source and the sustainer of the universe. He is not only Creator but also conserver of all that is. God is at once producer and provider of all living things. These roles depict his direct involvement in his world at all times from beginning to end.

God also has some indirect roles in creation. While he is the primary (first) cause of all things, he also works through secondary causes. What we commonly refer to as the processes of nature are God's indirect work through secondary or natural causes. In this capacity God is the remote cause, while natural forces are the proximate causes of events. God is the original commander, but he also works through a chain of commands when acting through natural laws.

God acts in his world in two ways: by direct intervention (as in the creation of the world) and by indirect action (as in preservation of the world). The first is an *immediate* act of God, that is, involving no mediating agent. The other is a *mediate* action, that is, some other being or force acts as God's agent. The direct acts of God are instantaneous; the indirect ones involve a process. God's acts of creation were discontinuous with what went before. He created *ex nihilo* (out of nothing). What he created is therefore *de novo* (brand new). He produced something from nothing, life from non-life, and the rational from the non-rational. These are discontinuities spanned by a direct act of God.

Further, God's acts of creation brought about unique events. Whereas, his acts of preservation involve a repetition of events. The one produced singularities, and the other produces regularities. The original creation events are unobserved today, but God's operation of the world can be observed in the present. God's actions can be contrasted like this:

Chart #1	God as:
Originator	Operator
Source	Sustainer
Creator	Conserver
Producer	Provider

Chart #2	God Working in Creation:
Working as:	**Working through:**
Primary Cause	Secondary Causes
Remote Cause	Proximate Causes
Ultimate Cause	Immediate Causes
Original Commander	Chain of commands

Chart #3	Results of God's Action:
Direct intervention	Indirect action
Immediate	Mediate
Discontinuous	Continuous
Unique event	Repetition of events
(Singularity)	(Regularities)
Unobserved	Observed

Causation, Nature, and Science

With this distinction between primary and secondary causes in mind, we are equipped to avoid two extremes among thinkers down through the centuries. On the one hand, some have yielded to the temptation to explain certain anomalous operations of the universe as miracles. Sir Isaac Newton explained the regular elliptical orbit of the planets as a divine intervention. Eventually, however, the astronomer Pierre Laplace provided a purely natural explanation for this phenomenon.[1] Many early Christians invoked divine intervention to explain geological processes. Eventually, the early geologists James Hutton and Charles Lyell were able to give satisfactory natural explanations for these phenomena. Before Charles Darwin it was assumed by many creationists that all species were fixed by a direct supernatural act of God. Likewise, earthquakes, meteors, and volcanoes were all once explained as divine interruptions of nature. The mistake in each case was to assume that the naturally unexplained functioning of nature was naturally unexplainable. This has been called the God-of-the-Gaps error. As it turned out, the gap was not really in the operation of nature but in the human understanding of it.

There is another equally mistaken view that may be called the Nature-of-the-Gaps error. This is not a mistake of supernaturalists but of naturalists. Here the temptation is not to interject a supernatural cause into the regularities of the world, but rather to assume there is always a natural cause for singularities in the world. But it is no more justifiable to presume there is always a natural cause for unexplained regularities in nature than it is to plead a direct supernatural cause for unexplained singularities. In fact, if an event is a continuous regular process, then by its very nature it can be assumed to have a natural cause. This is so even if we do not know what it is. On the other hand, an abrupt, discontinuous singularity or origin may have a supernatural cause. Usually we think of such a direct intervention by God in the natural order as a miracle. The key principle here is that although God normally works through secondary causes, we cannot therefore assume that he never works nor has worked directly on his creation.

Conclusion

We have seen that God's activity can be perceived in creating the world as well as in preserving it. He is both the originator and the operator of his universe. The acts of origin are always immediate acts of God as the first cause. However, in the continuance of the universe God has utilized the instrumentality of secondary causes. These we call natural causes because they are regular, observable, and predictable. They are the way God ordinarily operates in his world. The direct act of a first cause is different. It is the way God specially intervenes in his world. These are not regular nor predictable acts of God. Hence, we call these supernatural. These events have the same characteristics, whether they are the initial creation of something or subsequent miraculous events.[2]

The distinguishing characteristics of natural events are continuity, regularity, and predictability. None of these applies in the case of a miraculous origin event. It is wrong then to assume God miraculously intervenes continually in the ongoing natural processes of the world. Likewise, it is equally wrong to presume that a discontinuous, singular, and unpredictable event—like a miracle—must have a natural cause. God is involved directly as a supernatural cause for origins and indirectly through secondary causes in the operation of the world. He is both the Creator and the sustainer of all that he has made.

THREE

Spiritual Creation:
The Angels and Heaven

G OD CREATED NOT ONLY THE VISIBLE WORLD but also the "invisible" world (Col 1:16). More specifically, he created spiritual beings called angels. The account of creation in Genesis does not specifically mention the creation of the angels. Yet even a cursory study of the Bible, particularly the Old Testament, shows how God frequently uses angels as his agents and messengers. For instance, two angels literally dragged Abraham's nephew Lot and his family out of the wicked city of Sodom before it was destroyed by God (Gn 19:15-28). In the Gospel of Matthew, an angel of the Lord appeared to Joseph in a dream and told him to flee into Egypt with Jesus and Mary, because the wicked and jealous King Herod was seeking to destroy the child, who had been proclaimed the newborn king of the Jews by the wisemen (Mt 2:13-15). These examples and numerous others in the Scriptures make it clear that angels do exist.

The Creation of Angels

But what exactly are these agents and messengers of God that we call angels? First, angels have not existed eternally; they were created, just like the physical universe and

Angels Created

mankind. The psalmist declared, "Praise him, all his angels, praise him all his host! . . . For he commanded and they were created" (Ps 148:2, 5). Paul said of Christ Jesus, "In him were all things created, in heaven and on earth, visible and invisible, whether thrones or dominions or principalities or authorities . . ." (Col 1:16). Ezra exclaimed, "Thou art the Lord, thou alone; thou hast made heaven, the heaven of heavens, with all their host . . ." (Neh 9:6). The creation account in Genesis concludes that "the heavens and the earth were finished, and all the host of them" (Gn 2:1). Thus angels were probably created when the Scriptures say, "God created the heavens and the earth" (Gn 1:1). They were definitely created before the earth was, for they sang when the cornerstone of the earth was laid (Jb 38:7).

Nature of Angels

Angels are "spirits" (Mt 8:16; Heb 1:14). They do not have "flesh and bones" (Lk 24:39). They are called "spiritual hosts" (Eph 6:12). They are "invisible" by nature (Col 1:16), though some have assumed bodily form and appeared to men (Gn 19; Jgs 13). Angels are sexless beings (Mt 22:30). Hence, they do not reproduce their kind.[1]

Angels have free choice (1 Tm 3:6; Jude 6). Indeed, one third of all the angels God created used their free choice to follow Satan in his rebellion against God (Rv 12:4).

Angels are great in "wisdom" (2 Sm 14:20) and seek to know more about God's wonderful plan of salvation for mankind (1 Pt 1:12). Angels are also great in power (Gn 19:10-11; 2 Kgs 19:35). They are even called "sons of God" (Jb 1:6; 2:1). They are said to be "mighty in strength" (Ps 103:20). John the apostle refers to a "mighty angel" who will bring judgment on the world in the end time (Rv 10:1).

Like other rational creatures, angels have personality, including great intelligence, will, and even emotion. The latter is seen from the fact that they worship (Is 6:3), sing (Jb 38:7), and even "rejoice" when sinners repent (Lk 15:10). Like man, angels were created immortal. That is, even though they are creatures, they will live forever either blessed in God's presence (Lk 20:36) or banished from it (Mt 25:41).

Angels are beautiful creatures (Ez 1:4-17). When they appear their beauty is dazzling to behold (Dn 10:5, 6). The angel at Jesus' tomb had an appearance "like lightning, and his rainment [was] white as snow" (Mt 28:3). Even in his fallen state, Satan is able to appear as "an angel of light" (2 Cor 11:14).

There are special abilities possessed by angels, including traveling at great speeds (Dn 10:2, 12), performing miracles (Gn 19:11), and materializing (Gn 18:2, 8). They also have the ability to communicate with human beings, with God (Jb 1:6; 2:1), and with each other (Rv 7:1-3).

Moreover, just as there is a right ordering of relationships on the human and divine level for the sake of unity and the common good, so too there are orders of angels with various positions and functions to perform in worshiping God and serving God and man. We see this graphically displayed in the Bible.

Michael is called an "archangel" (Jude 9). There are other angels called "cherubim" (Ez 10:1) and "seraphim" (Is 6:2-3). Some angels of high rank are also referred to as "princes" (Dn 10:21). Throughout the description of heaven in the Book of Revelation, angelic beings—like the four living creatures—worship before the throne unceasingly, while others dispense God's judgment at the appropriate time (9:11; 9:14; 14:18; all of ch. 15; 16:5).

The Purpose of Angels

What is the purpose of angels? Like all of God's rational creatures, angels were created for God's glory. They sing (Jb 38:7; Rv 4:11), and "praise" God (Ps 148:2). Indeed, some angels continually sing "holy, holy, holy" in his presence (Is 6:3).

Like other creatures, angels were "created through him [Christ] and for him" (Col 1:16). They come regularly as "sons of God" to present themselves before the Lord (Jb 1:6; 2:1). They are constantly seen throughout the Bible running errands for God (Gn 18; Dn 10; Mt 1; Lk 1). In fact, one of their primary functions is as "ministering spirits sent forth to serve, for the sake of those who are to obtain salvation" (Heb 1:14). Believers are given guardian angels to help them throughout their life on earth (Ps 91:11; Mt 18:10). These guardian angels finally escort them into the presence of God (Lk 16:22). But most fundamentally, angels are God's servants. As his creatures all their service is for God's glory.

The Creation of Heaven

The angels dwell with God and the redeemed of humanity in the glory of heaven, which is also part of the "invisible" world (Col 1:17) created by God. Yet this understanding of heaven as the dwelling place of God with the angels and the redeemed is sometimes confused with two other meanings of heaven in the Bible, which have to do primarily with material creation. While we are mainly concerned with the understanding of heaven as part of spiritual creation, let's briefly define the other two meanings of heaven for clarity's sake.

The First Heaven. The atmosphere or the sky is the first heaven. It is referred to in Genesis 1:1. "In the beginning God created the heavens and the earth." Sometimes the first heaven simply means the sky above the earth. More specifically, it describes the atmosphere surrounding the earth as in Genesis 1:8 when "God called the firmament heaven."

We see other references to this understanding of heaven in the Book of Genesis. During Noah's time, we are told that "the windows of [the first] heaven were opened" (Gn 7:11) and the earth was flooded. Likewise, the builders of Babel wanted to construct a tower whose top would reach into the "[first] heavens" (Gn 11:4). And when God rained down fire and brimstone on the wicked in Sodom and Gomorrah, it fell "out of [the first] heaven" (Gn 19:24).

The Second Heaven. The Bible often speaks of the stars as "the hosts of heaven" (Gn 2:1; Dt 32:13). The Book of Judges says, "From heaven fought the stars, from their courses they fought against Sisera" (5:20). In these instances, Scripture is referring to outer space or the cosmos, which is the second heaven.

The second heaven is the arena of angelic conflict between the good angels and the demons—the bad angels who sided with Satan in his rebellion against God (Dn 8-9). It is here that Michael the Archangel fought with Satan (Jude 9). In fact, it is this sphere which is described as being under the dominion of the "prince of the power of the air" (Eph 2:2); that is, the devil.

The Third Heaven. In the Bible, the highest heaven is the "third heaven" (2 Cor 12:2), which is also called "paradise" (v. 3). This is the understanding of heaven we are primarily concerned about as part of spiritual creation. It is also the most common notion of heaven. Let's see how the Scriptures describe this meaning of heaven.

God himself reigns in the third heaven; it is his presence and rule that defines this heaven. As the psalmist expresses it, "The Lord's throne is in heaven" (Ps 11:4). Thus, "the Lord looks down from heaven upon the children of men..." (Ps 14:2). And again: "[The Lord] looked down from his holy height, from heaven the Lord looked at the earth" (Ps 102:19). In fact, this third heaven is the spiritual height of which David spoke when he said, "If I ascend to heaven, thou art there" (Ps 139:8). The third heaven is then the very presence and rule of God in the midst of his creation.

The Nature and Purpose of the Third Heaven

When Christians talk about "going to heaven" when they die, they are speaking of this third heaven. God created it for the good angels and the redeemed, just as hell was "prepared for the devil and his angels" (Mt 25:41).[2]

The Nature of Heaven. What exactly is heaven like? First, it is a place of eternal blessedness. Speaking to God, David declared, "In thy presence there is fullness of joy, in thy right hand are pleasures for evermore" (Ps 16:11). As Matthew records, Jesus will say to the faithful on Judgment Day, "Come, O blessed of my Father, inherit the kingdom prepared for you from the foundation of the world" (Mt 25:34). Thus the master tells his faithful servant in the parable of the talents, "Enter into the joy of your master" (Mt 25:21).

Heaven is also a place of absolute perfection. "Nothing unclean shall enter it, nor anyone who practices abomination or falsehood, but only those who are written in the Lamb's book of life" (Rv 21:27). Therefore, heaven is described as "clear as crystal," for no sin can dwell within its gates—but only the all-holy God, the good angels, and sinners who have been washed in the blood of the Lamb (Jesus) and clothed in "white robes" (Rv 7:9).

Since no sin can be found in heaven, the effects of sin are also noticeably absent. There will be no sorrow or crying in heaven: "[God] will wipe away every tear from their eyes, and death shall be no more, neither shall there be mourning nor crying nor pain any more, for the former things have passed away" (Rv 21:4). The redeemed will have physical but immortal resurrection bodies (1 Cor 15:12ff) without any aches or pains. These bodies will be like the resurrection body of Christ (Phil 3:20), the one who has gone on before the redeemed who will inherit the new creation.

Yet because we live in a fallen world wherein we experience the effects of sin, it is difficult for us to conceive of heaven. For it will be a glorious place of magnificent splendor beyond our wildest imaginings. John the apostle describes its pearly gates and streets of gold (Rv 21:9ff)— images of sumptuous wealth and glory that astonish the human mind. In Paul's vision of heaven, he mentions that "he heard things that cannot be told" (2 Cor 12:4). Even though Paul knew that God had revealed important heavenly truths to his people on earth, he stated clearly: "Eye has not seen, nor ear heard, nor the heart of man conceived, what God has prepared for those who love him" (1 Cor 2:9).

The desire of God to draw his chosen ones to himself in heaven is stated perhaps most profoundly by Jesus in the Gospel of John when he tells his disciples:

> "In my Father's house are many rooms; if it were not so, would I have told you that I go to prepare a place for you? And when I go and prepare a place for you, I will come

again and take you to myself that where I am you may be also." (Jn 14:2-3)

Thus we are "awaiting our blessed hope, the appearing of the glory of our great God and Savior Jesus Christ . . ." (Ti 2:13).

The Purpose of Heaven. The third heaven is a place of perfect bliss, but what is its primary purpose? As the Lord Almighty's dwelling place in the midst of the redeemed and the angels, it is a place of ceaseless praise and service to God. This is the primary purpose of heaven.

In God's awesome presence, the angels sing: "Holy, holy, holy is the Lord of hosts; the whole earth is full of his glory" (Is 6:3). The angels and the redeemed gathered round his throne to constantly praise God for his creation and his redemption. Of the creation, they sing: "Worthy art thou, our Lord and God, to receive glory and honor and power, for thou didst create all things, and by thy will they existed and were created" (Rv 4:11). Of God's redemption of his people, the heavenly hosts sing of the Lamb that was slain: "Worthy art thou to take the scroll and to open its seals, for thou wast slain and by thy blood didst ransom men for God from every tribe and tongue and people and nation, and hast made them a kingdom and priests to our God, and they shall reign on earth" (Rv 5:11).

Yet the purpose of heaven is not only the praise of God but also the service of him who is both Creator and Redeemer. We see this in the apostle John's description of the beatific vision. He says that "they [the redeemed] shall see his face, and his name shall be on their foreheads" (Rv 22:4). And note that John adds this important detail in the preceding verse: "His servants shall serve him" (v. 3 NIV).

Heaven is a spiritual place, then, of ceaseless worship and service of God. It is God's heavenly tabernacle, and his servants are a kingdom of priests (1 Pt 2:9) who ceaselessly serve him.

To sum up, the creation of the "invisible" world (Col 1:17) included the creation of both the angels and the third heaven. Heaven is the place where God dwells and rules over his creation. According to God's plan of creation and redemption, the good angels and the redeemed of mankind are called to worship and serve God in the perfect bliss and the indescribable joy of being united with God.

That is why earthly life is like a long engagement and heaven is the joyous "marriage feast of the Lamb." Thus John writes in the closing verses of Revelation: "The Spirit and the Bride say, 'Come.' And let him who is thirsty come, let him who desires take the water of life without price" (Rv 22:17).

Part Two

What Philosophy and Science Tell Us about Creation

FOUR

The Three Philosophical Views of Creation

WHAT ARE THE PRINCIPAL PHILOSOPHIES of life that have shaped the way creation is viewed? There are three main views: materialism, pantheism, and theism. Materi alists believe that everything comes out of matter (*ex materia*); pantheists claim that everything comes out of God (*ex deo*); and theists hold to creation by God out of nothing (*ex nihilo*). The Christian doctrine of creation is theistic. It can be understood more clearly by contrasting it with these other two positions.

Materialism: All Things Came Out of Matter

A materialistic view of creation contends that matter (or physical energy) is eternal. Matter always has been, and for that matter, always will be. The physicist claims, "Energy can neither be created nor destroyed." This is known as the first law of thermodynamics. The materialist applies this principle to the universe and concludes it is eternal. There are two basic subdivisions in the creation "out of matter" view: those that involve a God and those that do not.

1. Platonism: God Created out of Preexisting Matter.
Many ancients, including the Greeks, believed in creation by
God out of some previously existing, eternal "lump of clay."
That is, both God and the "stuff" of the material universe
(cosmos) was always there. "Creation" is the eternal process
by which God has been continually forming the matter,
giving shape to the stuff of the universe.

Plato held this view of creation out of matter.[1] He called
matter formless (or chaos). God was the Former (or
Demiurgos). Using an eternal world of forms or "ideas,"
God gave shape or structure to the formless mass of stuff
called matter. In brief, the Former (God), by means of the
forms formed the formless (matter) into the formed
(cosmos).

For Plato, and those who share his view, matter is eternal.
The basic stuff of the universe has always been here. There
never was a time when all the elements of the physical
universe did not exist. Everything has been forever. "Creation," therefore, means formation, not originating something out of nothing. God does not originate the matter; he
simply organizes the matter that has always been there. In
this Platonic view, the word Creator does not mean
originator of all that exists, but simply the builder. The
building blocks were already there. God just put them
together. Hence, God is only an architect of the physical
universe. He is not the source of all things.

A consequence of this view is that God is not really in
ultimate control of all things. For there is something eternal
outside of God. There is a given, something just there, and
even God must deal with it. Matter is just there, and he must
work with it. He can shape matter, but it places certain
limitations on him. Just as there are limits on what can be
made out of paper (it is good for making kites but not for

space ships), so the very nature of matter is a handicap to the Creator's ability. In short, both the existence and nature of matter place limits on God.

2. Atheism: Matter Is Eternal and Self-Forming. A second view within materialism is generally called atheism, although many agnostics hold it as well. An atheist says there is no God; an agnostic claims not to know whether there is a God. But neither believes it is necessary to posit God in order to explain the universe. Matter is simply there. In fact, for the atheist, the universe is ultimately all that exists. Even mind came from matter. If human beings have souls, the soul is dependent on the body as a shadow is on a tree. Once the body dies, the soul dies too, according to this view.

If questioned on where the universe came from, the strict materialist may ask in reply: where did God come from? For it makes no more sense to them to inquire who made the universe than to ask who made God.

That creation came out of matter has been held by many thinkers down through the centuries, from the ancient atomists (who reduced all things to atoms) to modern materialists like Karl Marx.[2] One of the most influential exponents of this view today is the astronomer Carl Sagan. He believes that "the Cosmos is all that was, is, or ever will be."[3] Man is simply stardust pondering stars. Rather than God creating man, man created God. As Karl Marx put it, mind did not create matter; matter created mind.[4]

Granting the eternal existence of matter and motion, the materialist explains everything else by purely natural evolution. Matter plus time, chance, and natural laws (such as natural selection) can explain everything. Even the complexities of human life are explained by the purely natural laws of the physical universe. No intelligent Creator is necessary.

If there is no Creator, then either the universe has always been, or—as one atheist put it—if matter came to be, it came into existence from nothing and by nothing.[5] The material universe is self-sustaining and self-generating. As Isaac Asimov speculated, there are equally good chances for either nothing to come from nothing or for something to come out of nothing. As luck would have it, something emerged.[6] So either matter is eternal or else it came from nothing spontaneously without a cause.

Traditional materialists believed there were innumerable indestructible little hard pellets of reality, called atoms. Since modern physics demonstrated the convertibility of mass and energy, materialists now speak of the indestructibility of energy. They appeal to the first law of thermodynamics, claiming that "energy can neither be created nor destroyed." Energy does not pass out of existence; it simply takes on new forms. Even at death, all the elements of our bodies are reabsorbed by the environment and reused by other things. So the process goes on forever.

In fact, atheism or nontheism is a logical outcome of strict materialism. That is, either there is no God or, at least, there is no need for a God. As the *Humanist Manifesto II* put it, "As non-theists, we begin with humans not God, nature not deity."[7]

No cause is needed to bring matter into existence or to form matter already in existence. The laws of nature suffice for both purposes. There is neither a Creator nor a former of the world. The world explains itself.

Among those holding creation out of matter there are differences regarding the nature of human beings. Most materialists accord a special status to humans as the highest point in the evolutionary process. However, virtually all agree that human beings are not qualitatively different from animals. Humans differ only in degree, not in kind, from lower forms of life. Human beings are the highest and latest animal form on the evolutionary ladder, but they are not uniquely different from other animals. They simply have some more highly developed abilities than primates.

Another implication of this view is that there is no immortal, never-dying "soul" or spiritual aspect to human beings. As *Humanist Manifesto I* noted, "The traditional dualism of mind and body must be rejected." For they believe that "modern science discredits such historic concepts as the 'ghost in the machine' and the 'separable soul.'"[8] The strict materialist does not believe in spirit or mind at all. There is no mind, only a brain. Thought is simply a chemical reaction in the brain. Thomas Hobbes in the seventeenth century defined matter as the whole of what exists:

> The world (I mean not the earth only, that denominates the lovers of it "worldly men," but the universe, that is, the whole mass of all things that are) is corporeal, that is to say, body; and hath the dimensions of magnitude, namely, length, breadth, and depth: also every part of body is likewise body, and hath the like dimensions; and consequently every part of the universe is body, and that which is not body is no part of the universe: and because the universe is all, that which is no part of it is nothing, and consequently nowhere.[9]

Less stringent materialists admit the existence of a soul but deny that it can exist independently of matter. For them the soul is to the body what the image in the mirror is to the one looking at it. When the body dies, so does the soul. When matter disintegrates, the mind is also destroyed.

Pantheism: Creation Out of God

On the other end of the spectrum from materialism is pantheism. Materialists claim all is matter; pantheists believe all is mind. On the subject of creation, materialists believe in creation out of matter (*ex materia*). But pantheism believes in creation out of God (*ex deo*). There are two basic categories into which pantheists fall: absolute pantheists, who deny the existence of matter entirely; and non-absolute pantheists who hold that matter is a kind of emanation, manifestation, or mode of God.

1. Absolute Pantheism. An absolute pantheist claims that only mind (or spirit) exists, not matter. What we call matter is only an illusion. It is like a dream or mirage. It appears to exist, but it really does not exist. There are two classical representatives of this view, Parmenides (a Greek) from the West and Shankara (a Hindu) from the East.

The Greek philosopher Parmenides argued that all is one, because to assume more than one thing exists is absurd.[10] If there were two or more things, they would have to differ. But the only ways to differ are by something (being) or nothing (nonbeing). However, it is impossible to differ by nothing, since to differ by nothing (or nonbeing) is just another way of saying there is no difference at all. Two things cannot differ by being because being (or existence) is the only thing they have in common. But it is impossible to differ by the very respect in which they are the same. Hence, Parmenides concluded, it is impossible to have two or more things. There can be only one being. All is one, and one is all. Thus whatever else appears to be does not really exist.

Put in the context of creation, this simply means that God exists and the world does not. There is a Creator but not really any creation. At least the only sense in which there can be said to be a creation is that it comes out of God the way a dream comes from a mind. The universe is only the nothing about which God dreams. God is the sum total of all reality. The nonreal about which he thinks and which appears to us, like zero, does not exist. It is literally nothing.

The Hindu philosopher, Shankara,[11] described the relation of the world to God, illusion to reality, by the relation of what appears to be a snake but on closer examination turns out actually to be a rope. When we look at the world, what is there is not reality (*Brahman*). Rather, it is merely an illusion (*maya*).

Likewise, when a person looks at himself, what appears to be (body) is only an illusory manifestation of what really is (soul). And when one looks into his soul, he discovers that the depth of his soul (*Atman*) is really the depth of the universe (*Brahman*). Atman (the human soul) is Brahman (God). To think we are not God is part of the illusion or dream from which we must awake. Sooner or later we must all discover that all comes from God, and all is God. So goes the pantheists' argument.

2. Non-Absolute Pantheism. Other pantheists, of whom there are a great many sorts, hold a more flexible and elastic view of reality.[12] While they believe all is one with God, they do not deny there is some multiplicity in the unity of God. They believe all is in the one as all radii are in the center of a circle or as all drops merge into one infinite pond. Representatives of this view include the Greek thinker and neoplatonist Plotinus, the seventeenth-century philosopher Baruch Spinoza, and the contemporary Hindu thinker Radhakrishnan.

According to this thinking there are many things in the world, but they all spring from the essence of the one (God).

The many are in the one, but the one is not in the many. That is, all creatures are part of the Creator. They come from him the way a flower unfolds from a seed or sparks come from a fire. Creatures are simply many drops that splash up from the infinite pond, only to eventually drop back in and blend with the rest. All things come from God, are part of God, and merge back into God. Technically speaking, for the pantheist, there is no creation but only an emanation of all things from God. The universe was not made out of nothing (*ex nihilo*), nor out of some preexisting matter (*ex materia*). It was made out of God (*ex deo*).

Even for moderate pantheists, there is no absolute distinction between Creator and creation. Ultimately Creator and creation are one. They may differ in perspective, as two sides of a saucer. They may differ relationally, as source does to sequent, as cause to effect. Creator and creation may be no more different than the reflection in a pond is to the swan swimming on it. One is a mirror image of the other that is the real thing. Even for those who believe the world is real, Creator and creation are simply two sides of the same coin. There is no real difference between them.

Pantheists believe that the relation between Creator and creation is eternal. God caused the world, but they insist that he has been causing it forever. Just as rays would shine forever from an eternal sun, or as radii always emerge from the center of an eternal circle, even so God has been creating forever. The universe is as old as God. Just as in an eternal world one stone could be resting on another forever, so the world could be dependent on God forever. So, according to pantheism, the cause has been creating from eternity.

Pantheists believe God and the world are of the same substance. Both are comprised of God-stuff. The creation is part of the Creator. It is one in nature with God. God is water. God is trees. As New Age writer Marilyn Ferguson put it, when one watches milk being poured into cereal, one sees God being poured into God![13] Ultimately there is only one substance, one stuff in the universe, and it is divine. We are all made of it, we are all God, according to this view.

If all of creation is the emanation of God, then so is mankind. The pop theologian of New Age pantheism, Shirley MacLaine, believes: "You can use *I am God*, or *I am Christ* or *I AM THAT I AM* as Christ did."[14] In her television program, "Out on a Limb," she waved to the ocean and proclaimed, "I am God. I am God!"[15] Lord Maitreya, believed by many to be the "Christ" of the New Age, declared through Benjamin Creme, his press agent, "My purpose is to show man that he need fear no more, that all of light and truth rests within his heart, that when this simple fact is known man will become God."[16]

Theism: Creation Out of Nothing

In contrast to both materialism and pantheism, stands the Judeo-Christian view of creation out of nothing. According to this position, God is above and beyond the world, not merely in it, and certainly not of it. The Creator is related to creation more like a painter is to a painting. The painter is not the painting, rather he created the painting and is manifest in it. Likewise, God is not the world. Rather, he created the world and manifests himself in it.

This position is represented by orthodox Judaism and Christianity. As Peter Kreeft noted, for Christians "The world is not God and not an illusion. In Eastern religions, the world is either God or an illusion, either part of God's mind or body, or *maya*, a trick."[17] Over the centuries, many Christian thinkers have not only defended the doctrine of creation on logical and biblical grounds, but have also developed and explored its philosophical consequences. These are radically different from those of materialism on the one hand or pantheism on the other. Perhaps the best way to demonstrate these differences is to examine some of their thinking, especially that of two of the most influential, the great Christian thinkers Augustine (354-430) and Thomas Aquinas (1224-74).

Concerning the creation, Augustine said three questions may be asked, "Who made it?, How? and Why? The answers are: 'God'; 'by the word'; and 'because it is good.'"[18] But what kind of God created the world? The answer to this involves many divine characteristics or attributes.

For instance, God is the "First Cause."[19] He is the "Beginning" beyond which there is no beginning. He is eternal and uncaused. He is indivisible and unchangeable.[20] He is infinitely wise and powerful. Further, God created voluntarily. As Aquinas observed in the *Summa Theologica*, "It is not necessary that God should will anything except Himself."[21]

Since God is a Trinity of Father, Son, and Holy Spirit, all three persons are involved in creation, as Aquinas concluded in his discussion on creation in the *Summa Theologica*. (See chapter note 21 for source information for this quote and following.)

> To the Father is appropriated power which is especially shown in creation. . . . To the Son is appropriated wisdom through which an intellectual agent acts. . . . To the Holy Ghost is appropriated goodness, to which belong both governance . . . and the giving of life.

Creation is ascribed to all three members of the Godhead

because in God his existence is identical with his essence and common to all three persons, and is, therefore, an activity of the whole Trinity, not peculiar to one person.

Not only did God create, but only God can create. For "to create is, properly speaking, to cause or produce the being of things," according to Aquinas. But only God can cause something to come into being. Man cannot create. "For an individual man cannot be the cause of human nature absolutely, because he would then be the cause of himself." In fact, "no created being can produce a being absolutely," reasoned Aquinas.

Since angels are also created beings, it follows that they cannot create. This is so since God alone is the primary cause and "no secondary cause can produce anything.... Hence it remains that nothing can create except God alone." Secondary causes do not create; they only reduplicate. As a "secondary instrumental cause does not share in the action of the superior cause.... so it is impossible for any creature to create." Thus Aquinas clearly distinguished between the creature and the Creator in his discussion on creation.

Implications of the Theistic View

We begin to see that the implications of a theistic view of creation contrast sharply with the materialistic and pantheistic views. Most strikingly, there is an absolute difference between the Creator and creation. As presented by Christian thinkers, this encompasses an entirely different view of origins. Theists believe that God created everything that exists—that there was no preexistent matter. God created existence out of nonexistence. He made something out of nothing. For Augustine the fact that God created all things "implies that before the creation of heaven and earth

God had made nothing."[22] But if there was nothing before God created, then ultimately he created everything out of nothing. "There could not have existed any matter of anything whatever unless it came from God, the Author and Creator of all that has been formed or is to be formed."[23]

1. Creation Is Not Out of God. While all things are from God, they are not of God.[24] Creation "is not out of Him, because it is not immutable, as He is." But since "it was not made of anything else, it was undoubtedly made out of nothing—but by Himself."[25] This does not mean that "nothing" is some sort of invisible stuff out of which God made the world. By "out of nothing" is meant "that it was not made from anything."[26] As Aquinas noted, the preposition "from" does not imply it came from something but simply that it followed after nothing. So creation from nothing is really creation after nothing. For "nothing is the same as no being."[27] But creation from nothing is not creation by nothing. Only what exists can cause, and only God can cause existence. God is existence by himself ("I AM WHO I AM," Ex 3:14); he alone produces everything else that exists.

2. God Created Out of Nothing. Out of what did God create? There is no material cause of creation. For between nothing and something there is no medium. Whatever comes from nothing must do so immediately and abruptly. There are no intermediaries between non-being and being. So "God produces being out of nothing according to the greatness of His power."[28] Since God has infinite power, he can do anything possible. It is not impossible for an infinite Creator to produce a finite creature. Thus God, who is existence, brought everything else into existence. Everything came from nothing but by someone. It takes power to produce something, but an infinite being has unlimited power, and unlimited power is not limited in its ability to create limited powers. God can create simply by "his word of power" (Heb 1:3).

God created not only by his power but also by his will. God is not bound by any obligation to create. Hence, "it is to be held with complete conviction that God brings creatures into existence of his own free will, and not as bound by natural necessity."[29]

3. The Universe Had a Beginning. In contrast to the other views of creation, theists hold that God is eternal but the world is not. The universe came to be but God always was. According to Aquinas, "That the world did not always exist we hold by faith alone; it cannot be proved demonstratively."[30] Others, like Bonaventure, a contemporary of Aquinas, held that it could be proven by reason that the universe had a beginning. Whatever our conclusion about this debate, all orthodox Christians acknowledge that the universe had a point of beginning. They all hold that it is temporal, not eternal.

Both time and space were created with the universe. There was no time before the world began, only eternity. God is prior to the universe in order but not in time, since there was no time before he created. For "things are said to be created in the beginning of time, not as if the beginning of time were a measure of creation, but because together with time the heavens and earth were created."[31]

Likewise, space was created with the world. For we hold that there was no place or space before the world was. Further, Augustine said, "It is silly to imagine infinite space since there is no such thing as space beyond the cosmos."[32] Neither was there any physical motion before there was a physical universe. However, "motion always existed from the moment that movable things began to exist."[33] God did not have to move to create motion nor did he need time to create time. Augustine asked: "Did the author of time need the help of time?"[34]

4. There Was No Time Before God Created. What was God doing before he created? Augustine had two answers, one humorous and one serious. First, he jests that God was preparing hell for those who ask such questions. More seriously he notes that there was no time before God created. For to speak of "doing" and "before" imply time. Hence, the question is as meaningless as: "What did God create before he created?" or, "What time is it for a timeless Being?" There is no time before time began, only eternity.

In view of the fact that time was created, it is senseless to ask how the eternal God occupied his time before he created time. For this same reason it makes no sense to ask why God did not create the universe earlier. For "earlier" implies there were moments before moments began. This is as meaningless as asking, "Why God did not create the world here rather than there?" For, as Augustine points out, "If they excogitate infinite periods of time before the world, . . . they ought to conceive of infinite reaches of space beyond the visible universe."[35] Since God created both time and space with the universe, there is neither time nor space beyond the universe. God neither created in time nor in space; rather, he created the universe with both time and space.

5. The Universe Is Not Eternal. If God did not create in time, then did he not create from eternity? And if he created from eternity, then is not the world eternal? All the orthodox Fathers rejected this conclusion, but some for different reasons. Aquinas believed eternal creation was theoretically possible (though not actually so).[36] This, he reasoned, is because, viewed "from above," God is eternal and an effect is simultaneous to its cause of existence. Bonaventure and others argued "from below" that an eternal universe is impossible because an infinite series of moments is actually unattainable. Both views agreed that the universe is not eternal.

The problem then is this: how can God be an eternal cause when the universe he caused is not eternal? In response it should be noted that the universe no more has to be eternal because God is eternal than it has to be infinite since he is infinite. Nor does it have to be necessary because God is a necessary being. The only thing a necessary being must will necessarily is the necessity of his own being. There is no necessity placed upon God to will the existence of contingent beings. Likewise, there is no reason an eternal being must will anything else to be eternal. While all material things flow from God's eternal will, he wills that all these things exist temporarily.

Everything preexists in God in accordance with his will. But God willed eternally that created things would have a beginning. Even though he willed them from eternity, nevertheless, they had a temporal beginning. For example, a doctor can decree from the beginning of his treatment that the patient take medicine later at successive intervals. Even so God can will events from all eternity that will occur at later successive times.

6. God Created to Communicate and Manifest His Goodness. If God created freely, then we can ask, "Why did he create in the first place?" Augustine's answer was, "Because it is good."[37] Aquinas concurs, saying, "God brings things into existence in order that his goodness may be communicated and manifested."[38] God is not required to share his goodness, but does so simply because he wants to. Commenting on the fact that God declared his creation was "very good" (Gn 1:31), Augustine concludes, "Surely, this can only mean that there was no other reason for creating the world except that good creatures might be made by a good God."[39]

7. Creatures Should Recognize and Thank God for His Goodness. God is infinitely good. As such he desires to share his goodness. Creatures should recognize the goodness God has showered upon them and thank him for it. In recognizing God's worth, they should attribute worth to him. Thus worship is the natural result of creation. Every rational creature—every man and woman and child, every angel—should worship the Creator. The purpose for creating is that the creature may worship God. "If he does not worship God, he is wretched."[40] As Augustine confessed, "Thou hast formed us for Thyself, and our hearts are restless till they find rest in Thee."[41] In brief, since a rational God created rational creatures, then it is only right and fitting that they should worship him. For in acknowledging his good as the highest good, they find their highest good. They find themselves in him and are satisfied.

It is important to recognize then that God and the world are radically different. One is the maker and the other is made. God is the cause and the world is the effect. God is unlimited, and the world is limited. The Creator is self-existing but creation is entirely dependent on him for its existence.

Creator	Created
Uncreated	Created
Infinite	Finite
Eternal	Temporal
Necessary	Contingent
Changeless	Changing

8. Every Created Thing Had a Beginning. Another crucial implication of the theistic view of creation from nothing is that the entire material and immaterial universe, (everything except God) had a beginning. Jesus spoke of his glory with the Father "before the world was made" (Jn 17:5). The world did not always exist. This does not mean that there was a time when the universe was not. Time began with the beginning of the world, and was there no time before time began. The only thing "prior" to time was eternity. That is, God exists forever; but the universe began to exist. Hence, he is prior to the temporal world ontologically (in reality), but not chronologically (in time).

To say that creation had a beginning is to point out that it came into being out of nothing. First it did not exist, and then it did. It was not, and then it was. The cause of its coming to be was God.

When the theist declares that God created "out of nothing" he does not mean that "nothing" was some kind of invisible, immaterial something that God used to make the material universe. Nothing means absolutely nothing. God alone existed and utterly nothing else. God created the universe and then, then alone, was there something else that existed. If "nothing" were really a hidden or secret something, then creation would really be out of something else (*ex materia*). Theists believe, on the contrary, in creation out of nothing (*ex nihilo*).

9. The Universe Did Not Come to Be from Nothing but Only by Someone. However, we should emphasize that creation out of nothing is not creation by nothing. Theism believes that the universe came to be from nothing but only by someone (God). It does not hold that nothing produced something. In fact, at the heart of the theistic belief in the causal power of God is a rejection of the premise that nothing can create something. Only something (or someone) can cause something. Nothing causes nothing.

We see then that the Christian doctrine of creation sets out to answer the same philosophical questions as the other two options. The table at the end of the chapter will summarize and focus the differences between the three positions. Properly speaking, materialism believes in natural generation; pantheism in eternal emanation; and only theism believes in supernatural creation. These are three very different views of the origin of the universe and man.

Christianity holds that since God brought the universe into existence, he is in sovereign control of it. God is infinite, necessary, and eternal. The creation is finite, contingent, and temporal. Hence, there is a real and radical difference between the uncreated Creator and the creation.

For theists, creation out of God is a contradiction in terms. For since God is eternal, infinite, and uncreated and the world is not, such a creation would be a temporal eternal, a finite infinite, and a created uncreated being. Thus, creation out of nothing makes it nonsense for a human being like Shirley MacLaine to say, "I am God." For it is impossible to have a dependent being that is necessary or a finite that is infinite. Such confusion of categories, which seems rampant today, is considered nothing short of sheer but deadly nonsense by thinking theists. As Paul said, we should "avoid . . . contradictions" like this that have caused some to stray from the faith (1 Tm 6:20).

Category	Theism	Materialism	Pantheism
Source of Creation	Creator beyond nature	No Creator	Creator within nature
Method of Creation	Out of nothing (*Ex Nihilo*)	Out of something (*Ex Materia*)	Out of God (*Ex Deo*)
Duration of Creation	Temporal	Eternal	Eternal
Relation of Creator and Creature	Creator and creation really different	No real Creator	No real creation
God's Control	Unlimited	Limited or nonexistent	Limited

FIVE

The Philosophical Arguments for Creation

THE TASK OF THE THINKING BELIEVER is to render the credible intelligible. For the believable must be rational. As Augustine said, "First believe, then understand."[1] It is our task here to offer a rational explanation for the Christian belief in creation. As we can see by examining the various doctrines of creation, belief in an eternal, infinite God as against a temporal, finite creation implies that this God created the universe. Therefore, most philosophical arguments for creation boil down to arguments for the existence of the Creator.

Since time immemorial rational creatures have offered rational arguments for the existence of God. Most of these fall into four broad categories: cosmological, ontological, teleological, and moral arguments. It is impossible to give a comprehensive survey of them here. The following, however, are representative of some of the more enduring forms of these arguments.

Cosmological Arguments

The cosmological argument is an argument from effect to

cause.[2] In one of its simplest forms it reasons:
1) Every effect has a cause.
2) The world (universe) is an effect.
3)Therefore, the world (universe) has a cause.

There are two forms of the cosmological argument, one arguing for a cause of the *beginning* of the world and the other for a cause of the present *being* of the world. The former was championed by Bonaventure and the latter by Thomas Aquinas. The first is based on "horizontal" causality and the latter on "vertical" causality. Since God is the originating cause and the sustaining cause of the universe, both arguments are appropriate. The argument for horizontal causality claims there must have been a cause to start the universe. It views God as an originating cause, like a finger pushing the first in a row of falling dominos. The argument for vertical causality insists on a cause to keep the universe in existence now. It is dependent on a simultaneous cause, like an image in a mirror that is simultaneously caused by the face looking into it.

The horizontal argument contends that the universe had a beginning and, hence, must have had a beginner. In brief it claims:
1) Every event has a cause to begin it.
2) The universe had a beginning.
3) Therefore, the universe had a cause.

Bonaventure offered several reasons for believing the universe is not eternal, most of which reject the possibility of an actual infinite series (of time, events, or things). One of the simpler forms of this argument goes as follows:[3]
1) An infinite number of moments can never conclude (there can always be one more moment in an endless series).
2) If there were an infinite number of moments before today, then today would never have arrived. For the present

moment would be the one that concludes this infinite number of moments.

3) But today has arrived.

4) Therefore, there were only a finite (limited) number of moments before today (that is, the world had a beginning).

The same kind of argument can also be used for a series of things or events. There can be a potential (abstract) infinite series but not an actual (concrete) infinite series. That is, no countable, enumerated series can be endless. For no matter how long it is, still one more thing (or event) can be added. But since nothing can be longer than an infinite series, therefore any series to which one can be added is less than infinite; it is finite. Thus, there must be a finite beginning of all time, events, or countable series of things. Since everything that begins has a cause, then the universe must have had a cause (i.e., God).

Others, such as Aquinas, expressed the vertical argument. They argue that the cause of here-and-now existence must be simultaneous with its effect.[4] Hence, they insist there must be a here-and-now cause of the finite universe in the present. While Bonaventure's argument follows God's role in beginning the universe, Aquinas's argument is about God's role in upholding the universe right now. Aquinas's argument can be summarized this way:

1) Every contingent (dependent) thing has a cause right now.

2) The whole universe is contingent.

3) Therefore, the whole universe has a cause right now.

In support of the second premise, the following is noted:

1) Every part (event) of the universe is presently dependent (caused).

2) The sum of all dependent parts (events) is also presently dependent.

3) Therefore, the sum total of the whole universe is presently dependent (or contingent).

This conclusion cannot be dismissed by claiming that the "whole" is more than and independent of the sum of all the parts. And if the "whole" is more than all the parts and independent from them, then it is the independent cause of all the parts. And if the whole is equal to all the parts, then the whole universe is contingent and needs an independent cause. In either case we are led from dependent things to an independent being on which they depend.

This reasoning can be stated another way. If the whole is equal to the parts then the whole would go out of existence if all the dependent parts did. Each and every dependent thing can cease to exist (that is precisely what a dependent being is, namely, one that can fail to exist). Hence, in this case everything could cease to exist so that absolutely nothing existed. If, however, there was ever absolutely nothing, then there would always be absolutely nothing, because nothing cannot produce something. It takes something to make something. Since there are some contingent beings, then there must always have been a necessary being on which they are dependent for their continued existence. Otherwise, nothing would be the cause of something, which is impossible. In summation:[5]

1) Something dependent presently exists.

2) Nothing cannot cause something.

3) Therefore, something necessarily exists.

Since a necessary being is one that cannot fail to exist, it not only exists now but always did and always will exist. In short, it is eternal. Further, since all contingent beings are finite, then a necessary being is not finite but infinite. And if it is infinite, then there can be only one, since two infinite beings are impossible. This leads to a discussion of the ontological arguments which begin with the idea of a necessary being.

The Ontological Argument

There are different forms of the ontological argument first offered by the Christian philosopher Anselm nearly a millennium ago.[6] The one most attractive to modern scholars can be stated like this:[7]

1) God is by definition a necessary being.
2) A necessary being is one that cannot not exist.
3) Therefore, a necessary being must exist.

The only way a necessary being can exist is necessarily. Just as a triangle by nature must have three sides, so a necessary being must necessarily be. For if a necessary existence could not exist, then it would be contingent and not a necessary existence. In short, if a necessary being can be, then it must be. Since there is no contradiction in the idea of a necessary being (like there is in a square circle), then such a being must exist.

The argument can be put in another form. A necessary being is a "must be." A contingent being is a "maybe," and an impossible being (square circle) is a "can't be." Now if a "must be" can be, then it must be. For a "must be" can't be a "maybe." So a "must be" kind of being must be.

The fascination of this argument notwithstanding, it has what some consider a fatal flaw.[8] This problem can be seen by analogy with a triangle. While it is true that triangles must have three sides, nonetheless, they do not have to exist outside the realm of pure thought. That is, if triangles exist then they must have three sides. But they do not have to exist. Likewise, if a necessary being exists, then it must necessarily exist. For the only way a necessary being can exist is to exist necessarily. But it is always possible that nothing ever existed, including a necessary being.

The response of the proponents of the ontological argument is to note that the statement "Nothing ever existed" is false because something does exist. For example, I exist. I cannot even deny that I exist without existing to deny it. Therefore, it is not actually possible (only theoretically possible) that nothing ever existed, including a necessary being. But if this is so, then the objection to the ontological argument fails and a necessary being must necessarily exist. This argument can now be summed up like this:

1) If something exists, then something necessarily exists.
2) Something does exist (for example, I exist).
3) Therefore, something necessarily exists.

What should be noted in this apparently valid form of the argument is that it is no longer an ontological argument. For an ontological argument begins with the *mere idea* of a necessary being. This argument starts with the *actual existence* of something (e.g., me). In fact, in attempting to make the reasoning valid it has been converted from a purely ontological argument to a cosmological argument. Rather than beginning with the mere idea of existence, it begins with actual existence and then argues to God. Many scholars are convinced that it is a valid argument for the existence of a necessary being.

The Teleological Argument

The teleological (from *telos*, "design, purpose") argument, like the cosmological argument, reasons from effect to cause. While the cosmological argument reasons from a finite (or dependent) effect, the teleological argument reasons from a designed or purposed effect. The most famous form of this argument was given by the eighteenth-century thinker William Paley in his watchmaker analogy.[9] Just as every watch has a watchmaker, even so the world has a world-Maker. For the world shows even greater design than a watch. In brief:

1) Every intelligent design has an intelligent designer.
2) The world manifests intelligent design.
3) Therefore, the world had an intelligent designer.

The criticisms of this argument fall into two broad categories. Some claim that the "design" in the world is the result of chance and evolution, not intelligence. Others insist that even if there is some kind of intelligent cause, it may be finite, or there may be even more than one. Hence, it is not identifiable with the Christian God.

In response to the latter argument, two things can be noted:

1) Since this is an ordered universe, a unified and interdependent whole, it argues for one unified cause of all.[10]

2) And since every finite thing needs a cause, the first cause must be infinite.

Of course, the teleological argument as such need not prove that the cause of the universe is infinite and one (this is done by the cosmological argument), but only that the cause is intelligent. Thus, the two arguments in concert reveal an infinite and intelligent cause of the world.

What about the "Enlightenment" thinker David Hume's argument that the whole universe could have resulted from chance?[11] After all, the chances for getting three sixes in throwing dice is only one in 216, but sometimes we get it on the first throw. Maybe the universe is simply a lucky shot in the dark.

In response to Hume's objection two things should be pointed out. First, while it is theoretically possible that everything happened by chance without any intelligent design, it is not very probable. One atheist, Sir Fred Hoyle,[12] calculated the odds for a one-cell animal to emerge by chance from non-living chemicals at one in 10^{40000}. This is like believing that a Boeing 747 resulted from a tornado raging through a junkyard. It is of course, theoretically possible, but it is actually incredible. Indeed, it is the implausibility of such a thesis that led Sir Fred Hoyle to discard his former atheism and to conclude life had an intelligent Creator.

A second point can be made to Hume's chance argument. It is contrary to Hume's own premise that credible belief in the cause of an effect is based on the constant conjunction of that cause with a certain kind of effect.[13] Put more simply, according to Hume, we can posit a certain kind of cause for a certain kind of effect only after we have seen similar ones regularly conjoined in our experience. Only what is uniformly connected can be rationally posited as a cause-effect relation. But if this is so then a purely chance explanation of the origin of life should be ruled out by Hume's uniformity principle. The kind of complex information found in a living cell is equal to that in a volume of an encyclopedia. But our regular, uniform experience informs us that such specified and complex information comes from an intelligent cause. For example, explosions in printing shops do not regularly produce encyclopedias. Nor do marbles randomly falling on a computer keyboard uniformly produce scientific research papers. Indeed, they never do. Even when we see a simple message like "Drink Coke" in the sky our previous experience of constant conjunction always leads us to posit an intelligent cause for it. Hence, by

Hume's own principle of constant conjunction, he should accept an intelligent Creator of life.

The Moral Argument

Like the cosmological and teleological arguments for God's existence, the moral argument reasons from effect to cause. Only in this case the effect is a moral law rather than a dependent being or an intelligent design. Since the time of the brilliant thinker Immanuel Kant[14] in the eighteenth century, there have been many forms of the moral argument.

The skeleton of most of the moral arguments goes as follows:

1) Every moral prescription has a moral prescriber.
2) There are absolute moral prescriptions.
3) Therefore, there is an absolute moral prescriber.

The first premise is self-evident. Prescriptive laws always have prescribers. All legislation has a legislator. But why cannot these moral laws be of purely human and subjective origin? Proponents of the moral argument have given many reasons why this is not plausible.[15]

First, the moral lawgiver must be beyond individual human beings. We often sense a conflict of our desires with the prescriptions of moral law. For example, I know I ought to love others even when I do not desire to do so.

Second, the moral law is beyond all humans for we collectively fall short of it. Judgments such as "All mankind is imperfect," or "The human race is not getting much better" make sense to us. In short, statements about better or worse make no sense unless there is a best by which they are measured. That is, we cannot say things are imperfect unless we presuppose a perfect scheme with which to compare them.

Third, we assume that statements like "Hitler ought not to have killed six million Jews" are not purely subjective. That is, it is not simply a matter of personal taste or opinion that genocide is wrong, but it is really wrong.

Fourth, unless there is an objective moral standard above and beyond subjective human feelings, then these absurd consequences follow:

1) No real moral disagreements have ever occurred; all arguments about right and wrong have been purely matters of subjective taste and opinion.

2) No moral judgment has ever been objectively wrong; indeed, each one was subjectively right.

3) Contradictions have occurred because opposite moral points of view have both been right.

4) No one should ever apologize for breaking any moral law (including vows, promises, and covenants). For none of them were really binding anyway.

The most popular modern form of the moral argument was given by C.S. Lewis in *Mere Christianity*[16] where he argued that:

1) This moral law cannot be the result of herd instinct or else the stronger impulse would always win, but it does not. Furthermore, moral law would always lead us to follow instinct rather than to oppose it (e.g., to place ourselves in danger to help someone in trouble), as we sometimes do. Finally, if the moral law is just herd instinct then herd instincts would always be in accordance with moral law, but they are not. Even love and patriotism are sometimes wrong.

2) That moral law is learned through society does not demonstrate it to be mere social convention because not everything learned through society is based on social convention (e.g., math or logic). Evidence of this is that the same basic moral laws can be found in virtually every society,

past and present. Furthermore, judgments about social progress would not be possible if society were the basis of the judgments.

3) The moral law is not to be identified with the laws of nature because the latter is descriptive (simply is), not prescriptive (ought) as moral laws are. Indeed, factually convenient situations (the way it is) can be morally wrong and vice versa. For example, someone who tries to trip me and fails is wrong, but someone who accidentally trips me is not.

4) Neither can the moral law be mere human fancy, because we cannot get rid of it even when we would sometimes like to do so. We did not create it; it is impressed on us from without. If it were fancy, then all value judgments would be meaningless, including "Hate is wrong" and "Racism is wrong."

If the moral law is not a description or a merely human prescription, then it must be a moral prescription from a moral prescriber beyond us. As Lewis notes, this moral lawgiver is more like mind than nature. He can no more be part of nature than an architect is identical to the building he designs.

The Argument from Evil

Other than those just mentioned, the main objection to an absolutely perfect moral lawgiver is the argument from evil or injustice in the world. No serious person can fail to recognize that all the murders, rapes, hatred, and cruelty in the world make it far short of being absolutely perfect. If the world is imperfect how can there be an absolutely perfect God? However, the only way the world could possibly be imperfect is if there is an absolutely perfect standard by which it can be judged to be imperfect. For injustice makes sense only if there is a standard of justice by which something is known to be unjust. Absolute injustice is possible only if there is an absolute standard of justice. As one former atheist put it:

> My argument against God was that the universe seemed so cruel and unjust. But how had I got this idea of just and unjust? A man does not call a line crooked unless he has some idea of a straight line. . . . Thus in the very act of trying to prove that God did not exist—in other words, that the whole of reality was senseless—I found I was forced to assume that one part of reality—namely my idea of justice—was full of sense. Consequently atheism turns out to be too simple.[17]

In brief, rather than disproving a morally perfect being, the evil in the world presupposes such an absolutely perfect standard. One could raise the question as to whether this ultimate lawgiver is all-powerful but not whether he is all-perfect. For if anyone insists there is real imperfection in the world, then there must be a really perfect standard of which this falls short.

Some argue that this all-perfect being cannot be all-powerful simply because he has not yet defeated evil. This objection prejudges the issue. The only thing we know is that evil is not *yet* defeated; God may yet be victorious over evil. Indeed, if he is all-perfect, then he wants to defeat evil. If he is all-powerful he can defeat evil. Hence, since evil is not yet defeated we can be sure it will one day be defeated. For an all-perfect and all-powerful God has both the desire and the ability to defeat it.

The Value of Rational Arguments

Do these rational arguments prove that God exists? What is their purpose? Is their value in them for believers or unbelievers? A brief response to these and like questions is in order.

Rational arguments offer proof but do not necessarily persuade unbelievers of God's existence. They may be objectively correct but not always subjectively convincing. This is because they are directed at the mind but are not directive of the will. They can "lead the horse to the water," but only the Holy Spirit can persuade a person to drink. This does not mean arguments are without value. For if rational beings are to make rational decisions they should have rational evidence. At best, however, they are objective proofs, not as such subjectively persuasive. They provide reasons for the mind but do not regulate the will.

The fact that rational arguments do not always persuade unbelievers is not necessarily a flaw of the arguments. For belief in God involves the will as well as the mind. Arguments can help unbelievers perceive the truth, but they must receive it (1 Cor 2:14). Such arguments, however, can play an important role in preparing a person for making a rational choice to believe in God. For belief that God exists is logically prior to belief in God. No rational person boards an airplane without some prior evidence that it can fly safely. He needs evidence that a safe plane exists before he places trust in it. Likewise, thinking persons do not get on an elevator unless they have evidence there is a floor on it. Again, evidence that something exists is prior to belief in it. In like manner, good reasons for believing that God exists are logically prior to placing one's faith in God. The former is an act of the mind and the latter of the will.

It should be emphasized, however, that belief that God exists (or that Christ is Savior) is not sufficient for salvation. The "demons believe that" there is a God (Jas 2:19) and they are forever lost. Thus all the rational arguments in the world cannot, as such, lead one to salvation. Only the blessed Holy Spirit can do that. Arguments can convince the head, but only the Holy Spirit can persuade the heart.

Of course, God wants to reach the heart, but not at the expense of the head. Christianity is not a leap of faith in the dark. Rather, it is a step of faith in the light—in the light of good reasons. Thus it is most appropriate, as the apostle Paul did, to reason with unbelievers (Acts 17:2, 17). Indeed God has given such "plain" evidence that they are "without excuse" (Rom 1:19-20) if they reject it. The fact of creation, which is evident to all men, makes their unbelief inexcusable.

There is a legitimate role for reason prior to faith. As Augustine said:

> For who cannot see that thinking is prior to believing? For no one believes anything unless he has first thought that it is to be believed. . . . Although even belief itself is nothing else than to think [reason] with assent.[18]

But there is also a proper role of reason subsequent to faith in God. For not only is faith the step of understanding but understanding is the reward of faith. Hence, one cannot only reason to God but also for God. That is, once one has believed in God he can find reasons for that belief. He can love the Lord with all his mind, as well as his heart (Mt 22:37). Indeed, it is of the essence of a thinking faith that it render the credible more intelligible. (Of course, it is not wholly comprehensible to us because we are finite creatures.)

Rational explanations of creation and the Creator are crucial for a rational creature. Making sense out of faith in God is as important after believing as it is before. Christianity not only says, "Look before you leap," but it also believes in rationally exploring the new realm to which the step of faith has brought the believer. The Christian says, "I believe for good reasons, and then I explain my belief with good reasons."[19] Hence, a rational explanation of God's creation is part of the rational creature's duty to his Creator.

Conclusion

In summary, then, the cosmological argument shows there is an infinitely powerful and eternally necessary being. The teleological argument reveals that he is incredibly intelligent. And the moral argument manifests that he is morally perfect. Together they give rational support for the Christian belief that there is a Creator and sustainer of all things who is also the moral lawgiver to all rational beings.

Of course, not everyone will be persuaded by these arguments. Proof is a matter for the mind; persuasion is a matter of the will. At least the rational arguments provide evidence that God exists, which is logically prior to belief in God. They offer a rational look before they call for an existential leap. The truth about God does not bypass the mind on the way to the heart. It opens a way from the mind to the heart for the true seeker.

SIX

Science and Creation

G OD CREATED ALL THINGS "visible and invisible" (Col 1:16). Both the physical and the spiritual worlds were created by God, matter as well as spirits. The material world is known as the space-time universe, the cosmos. It also contains a multitude of living creatures. These physical and biological worlds are the object of scientific enquiry. Since science has assumed the role of speaking about the origin of the universe and living things, it is unavoidable to discuss the doctrine of creation from a scientific point of view.

Like mountain climbers approaching the same peak from two different vantage points, both scientist and theologian approach the origins of the universe in different ways. The theologian begins with Scripture and the scientist begins with the physical world. The former begins with God's Word and the latter with God's world.

The roots of modern science are firmly planted in the Christian view of creation. The twentieth-century philosopher Alfred North Whitehead observed: "The faith in the possibility of science, generated antecedently to the development of modern scientific theory, is an unconscious derivative from medieval theology."[1] M.B. Foster, writing about the origin of modern science asked,

> What is the source of the un-Greek elements which were imported into philosophy by the post-Reformation philosophers . . . ? [And] . . . what is the source of those un-Greek elements in the modern theory of nature . . . ? The answer to the first question is: The Christian revelation, and the answer to the second: The Christian doctrine of creation.[2]

Most of the early founders of modern science believed in creation. The great scientist-philosopher Francis Bacon pointed to the creation mandate in Genesis 1:28 as the impetus for scientific research.[3] Indeed Galileo, Copernicus, Kepler, Kelvin, Newton, and others all saw evidence in nature for creation. After carefully studying the universe, Newton concluded:

> It is not to be conceived that mere mechanical causes could give birth to so many regular motions, . . . This most beautiful system of the sun, planets, and comets, could only proceed from the counsel and dominion of an intelligent and powerful Being.[4]

From the very beginning of modern science there was a belief in a Creator (first cause) who created the universe and then operated in it by natural laws (secondary causes).[5] The study of these regular ways God operated in his universe produced astounding results. More and more scientists were able to give natural explanations for things once believed to be the result of direct supernatural intervention.[6]

Laplace and Kant before him provided a naturalistic explanation of the development of the solar system. Laplace corrected Newton's misbelief that God intervened to correct the elliptical orbits of planets. Hutton and Lyell explained geological processes by natural causes apart from supernatural interference. Darwin later offered a natural explanation for the emergences of species. Gradually, this widely accepted success in explaining the operation of the natural world overshadowed the question of its ultimate origin. The search for secondary causes obscured the need for a primary cause.[7] Theism degenerated to deism and set the stage for atheism.

Departure from the Creator was not envisioned by the early modern scientists. In their view the primary cause was needed both directly (for the origin of the universe and living things), and indirectly (for the operation of the world) through secondary causes. It was not their intention that secondary (natural) causes should be used to eliminate the need for a primary cause (Creator), in the realms either of the origin of or the operation of the universe and living things. Forgotten was the two-fold need of a primary cause as the immediate originator of the universe and all living things, and as the sustainer of all secondary (mediate) causes in the operation of the universe. That this great divide has opened up between primary and secondary causes in the modern scientific world is a tragedy of enormous proportions. Man has lost his bearings and has ended up confused and bewildered.

Origin and Operation Theories

The failure to make this distinction between the origin and the operation of the universe has led to much confusion. A good example is in the ongoing debate between creationist and evolutionist. The latter often claim that evolution is a well established scientific fact and that creation is not scientific. This, however, confuses two kinds of scientific theory so different they might be called different kinds of science: origin science and operation science. Operation science is an empirical science. Origin science is more like a forensic science. Operation science deals with present regularities, but origin science deals with past singularities. The latter deals with the origin of the universe and life; the other deals with its functioning in the here and now.

The crucial difference is that in operation science there is a recurring pattern of events against which a theory can be tested. In origin science there is not, for it deals with a past singularity. Hence, there is no direct way to test a theory or model of origin science. It must be judged as plausible or implausible on the basis of how consistently and comprehensively it reconstructs the unobserved past from evidence available in the present.

The basic principles of these two kinds of science are also different. Operation science is based on observation and repetition. The laws of physics and chemistry, for example, are based on the observation of recurring patterns of events. Such observations can be made with the naked eye or with the aid of instruments, such as the telescope and microscope. There must be some repetition of each pattern, for no scientific projection can be made on the basis of a singular event. Operation science is thus based on the repetition of similar patterns of events that make it possible to account for present regularities and project future ones. No scientific prediction, however, can be made from a singular event. It takes a series or pattern of events before a valid projection can be made.

Origin science, on the contrary, is not based on either the observation or the repetition of the events of origin. It deals with unobserved past singularities, such as the origin of the universe and the origin of life. Since no human being was there to observe the origin of life, that is not the proper subject of operation science. The operation of the cosmos, for example, belongs to the science of cosmology. But the origin of the cosmos belongs to the science of cosmogony. The latter deals with the genesis of the world; the former treats its operation. Properly speaking, the science of biology does not deal with the beginning of life but with its continual functioning since its origin. How life began is biogeny; how it continues is biology. Basically then, there are two kinds of science.

Two Kinds of Science

Category	Origin science	Operation science
Object of science	Past singularities Beginning of universe	Present regularities Running of universe
Kind of science	Forensic science	Empirical science
Principles of science	Causality Analogy	Observation Repetition
Areas of science	Cosmogony Biogeny Anthropogeny	Cosmology Biology Anthropology

It is important to note that the laws by which something operates are not the same as the cause(s) by which it began.

For example, the laws necessary for running a windmill are not sufficient to produce one. A windmill functions by purely natural laws of physics (pressure, motion, inertia, etc.). However, these natural laws do not create windmills; they only explain how they operate. The reason for this is that natural laws deal with the continuation of things, but they are not sufficient to explain their commencement.

It is only because things operate in a regular way in the present that it is possible to make observations and predictions based on them. Thus both observation and repetition are necessary for natural (operational) science. The origin of past events, whether of the universe or of life, was not observed and is not repeated. Hence, it does not fall under the domain of natural (operational) science. Since an origin event is by its very nature not repeated, it falls into a class of its own. It is an unobserved singularity. It has not happened again. Hence, it must be approached in a different way than empirical science does.

Actually, origin science is more like a forensic science. Forensic science is involved where there is no observation of the actual event, and it cannot be repeated. For example, take the case of an unobserved death by an unknown cause. A detective is called in to apply the principles of forensic science to solve the case. Was it murder or suicide? Since no one saw it, the detective knows that the principle of observation used in operation science won't help solve the case. Since the victim is dead it cannot be repeated. All the detective has is some evidence which he hopes will help him reconstruct the murder or suicide as it actually happened.

Lacking the principles of empirical science does not totally frustrate the detective's scientific analysis of how the person died. For the principles of forensic science can help him to solve the case. Using the evidence that remains (such as weapons, wounds, finger prints, etc.), the forensic scientist can make a speculative but plausible reconstruction of the original event. In a similar way, the origin scientist attempts to reconstruct past unobserved singularities, such as the origin of the universe and the origin of life.

The Principles of Origin Science

Every discipline has its own principles. Operation science is based on observation and repetition. Without a recurring pattern of events against which to measure theories, there is no valid operational science. But since origin science lacks both observation and repetition of origin events, it must depend on other principles. Besides the two obvious principles of consistency and comprehensiveness that every theory or model should employ, the most crucial principles of origin science are causality and uniformity (analogy).[8]

The Principle of Causality. Like the forensic scientist, the origin scientist believes that every event has an adequate cause. This is true of unobserved events as well as observed ones. This principle has a venerable history in science and scarcely needs justification. It is sufficient to note that Aristotle said, "The wise man seeks causes." Francis Bacon believed that true knowledge is "knowledge by causes."[9] Even the skeptic David Hume said, "I never asserted so absurd a proposition as that anything might arise without a cause."[10] It is self-evident to most rational beings that everything that comes to be had a cause. Nothing does not produce something. If something came into existence, then something caused it. Indeed, without the principle of causality, there would be no science of operation or origins. Whether in the past or present, everything that begins has a cause.

It is important to note that the principle of causality does not claim that everything has a cause. For with the atheist we would agree that if matter (energy) is eternal and indestructible, then it does not need a cause. That is, if it is literally true that "energy can neither be created nor destroyed," then this kind of energy would not need a cause; it would be uncaused. Atheists have long believed that the universe (cosmos) is eternal—without beginning. If this were so, then it would be possible that the universe does not have a cause. We say that everything has a cause; but we mean that everything that begins does have a cause. Or, more properly, the principle of causality does not apply to everything but only to:

1) everything that begins;
2) everything that is finite;
3) everything that is contingent or dependent.

That is, every event needs a cause but every thing does not. If there is some thing (being) that is eternal and independent (whether it is the universe or God), then it does not need a cause. Causality applies to things that come to be, not to what simply is but never came to be. Whatever just is, does not need a cause; it is uncaused. The question to be answered is whether the cosmos (space-time universe) came to be (as Christians and other theists hold), or whether it always was (as many noncreationists believe).

The Principle of Uniformity. There is another principle of origin science. Broadly speaking, it is known as the principle of uniformity (or analogy).[11] Generally stated, it affirms that "the present is the key to the past." Applied more specifically to the question of past unobserved causes, the principle of uniformity (analogy) asserts that the kind of cause that regularly produces certain kinds of events in the present is the kind of cause that produced a like effect in the past. Or more briefly, past events have causes similar to the causes of like present events.

There are several things to note about the principle of uniformity. First, it derives its name from the uniform experience on which it is based.[12] That is, repeated observation reveals that certain kinds of causes regularly produce certain kinds of events. For example, water flowing over small rolling rocks has a rounding effect. Wind on sand (or water) produces waves. Heavy rain on dirt results in erosion, and so on. All of these causes are natural or secondary ones. That is, their effects are produced by natural forces whose processes are an observable part of the ongoing operation of the physical universe.

Besides secondary causes, there is another kind of cause known as a primary (first) cause.[13] Intelligence is a primary cause. The principle of uniformity (based on constant conjunction) informs us that certain kinds of effects come only from intelligent causes. Human language, arrowheads, pottery, portraits, and symphonies all have intelligent causes. So convinced are we by previous repeated experience that only intelligence produces these kinds of effects that when we see even a single event that resembles one of these kinds of effects we invariably posit an intelligent cause for it.

For example, when we see "Buy Fords" written in the sky, we never assume it was placed there by a secondary cause like wind and clouds. Likewise, when we see the faces of presidents on Mount Rushmore, we conclude that some intelligence caused them. And when we come across "John loves Mary" written on the beach, we never assume the waves did it. The reason we unhesitatingly posit intelligent causes for these kinds of things is that we have repeatedly observed that similar kinds of effects are produced by intelligent causes.

It comes down to this question about the origin of the first living organism (which we did not observe): Was it caused by a non-intelligent pure natural cause or an intelligent cause? The only scientific way to determine this is by analogy with our experience of what kind of cause regularly produces that kind of effect in the present.

Another thing to observe about the principle of uniformity is that it is an argument from analogy. It is an attempt to get at the unknown (past) through the known (present). Since we do not have direct access to the past, we can "know" it only by analogies with the present. This is how human history is reconstructed, and it is the way earth history and life history are recreated as well. Historical geology is a case in point. It is totally dependent as a science on the principle of uniformity. Unless we can presently observe in nature or the laboratory certain kinds of causes producing certain kinds of events, we cannot validly reconstruct geological history. But since we can observe natural causes producing these kinds of effects today, we can postulate that similar natural causes produced similar effects in the geological record of the past.

The same point can be made for human history where primary intelligent causes are involved. Archaeology as a science is possible only because we assume the principle of uniformity. Thus when we find certain kinds of tools, art, or writing, we posit intelligent beings who produced them. Even simple arrowheads lead us to claim Indians produced them, not natural forces, such as wind and water. When past remains contain writing, art, poetry, or music, we have no problem whatsoever in insisting on intelligent primary causes for them. So whether it is a secondary or primary cause that is called for, the principle of uniformity is the basis. For unless we have a constant conjunction of a certain kind of cause with a certain kind of effect in the present, then we have no grounds on which to apply the principle to past events known only from their remains.

Now that we have an understanding of the basic principles of origin science, let us apply them to the three main areas of origin: the beginning of the universe, the emergence of first life, and the appearance of human (rational) beings. In each of the areas of the origin of the cosmos, life, and man, we will try to determine whether the scientific evidence favors positing the direct action of a primary cause or a secondary cause for these events. The two principles used to determine this will be the principle of causality and the principle of uniformity (analogy). The question is this: was the cause of the origin event a purely natural cause or an intelligent one? Or to put it simply, did God create the universe? If he didn't, what or who did? Did it all *simply* start with a big bang without God?

The Origin of the Universe

The Christian doctrine of creation states that there was a beginning of the universe. The universe is not eternal; it came into existence out of nothing. The question here is whether there is any scientific evidence to support this belief.

The Scientific Evidence. There are several lines of evidence that convince even agnostic scientists that the universe came into existence out of nothing. One of the most important is the second law of thermodynamics, which states: *the amount of usable energy in the universe is decreasing.* Another way to put it is that in the universe as a whole things are generally moving from order to disorder. Energy can only move by itself from a more to a less energetic state. As the energy generated in each star dissipates into space, the various parts of the universe become more uniform, and less energy can be transferred from one part to another.

According to this scientific law, local systems or smaller areas of the universe are open systems that receive energy from outside them. A living organism, for example, receives outside energy (from the sun) that keeps it from going into disorder and using up its energy. Since the universe as a whole is a closed system, there is no outside source of physical energy to help it overcome the degenerating effects of the second law of thermodynamics. Hence, the universe as a whole is running down. But if it is running down, then it is not eternal. If the universe were infinite, it would not be running down: an infinite amount of energy cannot run out. In short, whatever is petering out must have had a beginning because it does not take forever to run out of a limited amount of energy. So the second law of thermodynamics points to a beginning of the universe.

Looking at this issue, the astrophysicist Dr. Robert Jastrow, concluded that "three lines of evidence—the motions of the galaxies, the laws of thermodynamics, and the life story of the stars—pointed to one conclusion; all indicated that the Universe had a beginning."[14] If so, then this is scientific support for the Christian doctrine of the creation of the universe. For it is a rational inference based on scientific evidence that the physical universe is not eternal. Rather, it came into being. Whatever comes to be needs a cause; so it is reasonable to posit a Creator of the physical universe.

Most contemporary astronomers believe that the universe is expanding. They believe this because measurements indicate that stars are moving apart. No matter where they look in the sky, the distant galaxies are moving away from the earth; and the further away the galaxy, the faster it is receding. If these observations and inferences are correct, then they are further confirmation that the cosmos had a point of beginning. For if one reverses the "camera" of time, the universe gets smaller and smaller until it is invisible. Indeed, if it is carried back mathematically and logically, one reaches a point where there is no space, no time, and no matter. There is literally nothing. So there was nothing and then suddenly there was something out of nothing.

Needless to say, if the universe had a beginning, as many scientists are now claiming, this is a striking scientific confirmation of the Christian belief in creation out of nothing (*ex nihilo*). Indeed, even many nontheistic astronomers and scientists are speaking of "creation out of nothing." Some who want to avoid God are claiming that "the universe came into existence from nothing and by nothing." This, however, is a denial of the principle of causality and is contrary to the very nature of science which is to find an adequate cause for events. It does, however, show that the evidence for the universe coming into existence out of nothing is so persuasive to them that they have had to stop positing an eternal and therefore uncaused universe. They cannot now rationally avoid the thought of a Creator.

A third line of evidence has convinced many scientists that the universe had a beginning. Two scientists, Arno Penzias and Robert Wilson, were given a Nobel prize in 1978 for the discovery of the radiation fireball.[15] The entire universe is giving off a radiation glow the exact wavelength of that produced by a gigantic explosion. They postulate that this would have been the result of the "Big Bang" when the universe exploded on the scene some billions of astronomical years ago.

The evidence for the expanding universe shows that the universe expanded faster in the past, and this fits with the concept of an explosion which produces greater velocities at first but later slows down and eventually peters out. The data from the second law of thermodynamics indicates that the universe is running down. Thus the three lines of evidence converge to show that the cosmos had a beginning—exactly the point of the biblical teaching about creation. Indeed, the agnostic astronomer, Robert Jastrow, declared that: "Science has proven that the universe exploded into being at a certain moment." So he concluded, "The scientist's pursuit of the past ends in the moment of creation."[16] If the universe was created, then it is reasonable to posit a Creator for it.

However, for several reasons this scientific evidence is not full proof that the physical universe had a beginning. First, scientific evidence by its nature does not yield full proof of things, except on a very limited, material level in some controlled situations. Second, other more satisfactory explanations may be found for the expanding universe and the radiation. Some have even suggested that the second law of thermodynamics does not apply to the whole universe but only to closed isolated systems within it. Most often they suggest a rebound theory: the universe will bounce back from its expansion and start over again, and so on infinitely. Although this view lacks convincing evidence, it does show that one must temper dogmatism about scientific arguments. Perhaps it is simply sufficient to say that the prevailing view in the scientific community presents evidence that strongly supports what Christians have always believed on biblical (and some even on philosophical) grounds, namely, that the universe had a beginning.

Now if the existing evidence supports the view that the cosmos came into existence out of nothing, then it is reasonable to posit a cause for it. Since the cosmos is the natural universe, then by its very nature, as a cause beyond the natural world, this first cause would be a supernatural cause. This is, of course, what Christian theists have always affirmed; namely, "In the beginning God created the heavens and the earth" (Gn 1:1).

The Origin of First Life. The Bible declares that "God created every living creature" (Gn 1:21). By contrast, the prevailing theory among scientists is that life began by spontaneous generation from nonliving chemicals. As a matter of fact there are only two possible views: either life was originated by an intelligent Creator, or else it resulted by purely natural processes from nonliving matter. As Robert Jastrow put it, "Either life was created on the earth by the will of a being outside the grasp of scientific understanding, or it evolved on our planet spontaneously, through chemical reactions occurring in nonliving matter lying on the surface of the planet."[17]

Which view of the origin of life is more scientifically plausible? Before answering this, we must remind ourselves that in origin science there is no direct observational way to measure our theory against the original event itself (of the emergence of first life). For no scientist observed the origin of life, and it is not being repeated over and over again. Ever since the work of the seventeenth-century naturalist Francesco Redi's and French chemist Louis Pasteur's experiments in the nineteenth century, the theory of spontaneous generation of life in the present has been discredited. In spite of this, many scientists speculate that life in the past arose spontaneously contrary to all evidence in the present. This, of course, is a violation of the principles of uniformity and causality by which theories of origin are tested. Since the second of these principles says there must be an adequate cause, we have to ask, what kind of cause is adequate to explain the origin of life?

The principle of uniformity (analogy) declares that the kind of causes that produce certain kinds of effects in the present should be posited for these kinds of effects in the past. That being so, the question is: what kind of effect takes the direct action of an intelligent cause and what kind takes only a natural cause? We know by observing constant conjunction in the present that natural causes can and do produce sand dunes but that it takes intelligent causes to produce sand castles. Likewise, natural causes make crystals, but only intelligent causes create chandeliers. The chart on the following page will further clarify this distinction.

When looking at these two lists we know immediately that natural causes alone never produce the kinds of effects in the right hand column. But why? The answer is the principle of uniformity. Our uniform experience, based on constant conjunction of intelligent causes with these kinds of effects, leads us to believe that other similar effects will also have an intelligent cause. If this is the case, we need only ask: is a living cell more like an encyclopedia or a bowl of alphabet soup?

Definitions of biological life are hard to come by.[18] However, some distinguishing characteristics are clear. The

Natural Cause Produces	Intelligent Cause Produces
sand dunes	sand castles
crystals	chandeliers
waterfalls	power plants
round stones	arrow heads
Mt. McKinley	Mt. Rushmore
clouds	sky writing
arrangements of letters in alphabet soup	arrangement of letters in an encyclopedia

famous biologist Leslie Orgel observed the important differences when he said, "Living organisms are distinguished by their specified complexity. Crystals . . . fail to qualify as living because they lack complexity; random mixtures of polymers fail to qualify because they lack specificity."[19] That is to say,

a. Crystals are specified but not complex;

b. Random polymers are complex but not specified;

c. Life is both specified and complex.

In brief, life on the genetic level is characterized by specified complexity. What this means can be understood by the concept of boundary conditions. The famous biologist

Michael Polanyi explains:

> When a saucepan bounds a soup that we are cooking, we are interested in the soup; and, likewise, when we observe a reaction in a test tube, we are studying the reaction, not the test tube. The reverse is true for a game of chess. The strategy of the player imposes boundaries on the several moves which follow the laws of chess, but our interest lies in the boundaries—that is, in the strategy, not in the several moves as exemplification of the laws. And similarly, when a sculptor shapes a stone or a painter composes a painting, our interest lies in the boundaries imposed on a material, and not in the material itself.[20]

Life is made up of a (four-letter) genetic alphabet that manifests the characteristics of intelligently imposed boundaries or conditions, such as a skywriter imposes on smoke, a potter on clay, or an author on letters. In fact, studies done by contemporary biologist Herbert Yockey on the application of information theory developed for human language reveal that the pattern sequence in the genetic code and that in a human language are "mathematically identical." Yockey concludes: "The sequence hypothesis applies directly to the protein and the genetic text as well as to written language and therefore the treatment is mathematically identical."[21] What does this tell us about the author of the genetic text inside our *own cells*?

Is life more like a bowl of alphabet soup or an encyclopedia? It is exactly like an encyclopedia. In fact the genetic information in a single-cell animal, if spelled out in English, is equal to that of a whole volume of the *Encyclopedia Britannica*. In spite of his confessed agnosticism, Carl Sagan provides powerful proof for an intelligent Creator of life when he argues that "a single message"[22] from outer space would prove to him that there is supernormal intelligence behind it. If one short message takes super-human intelligence, then how much more would a whole volume of an encyclopedia? The American astronomer Allan Sandage said it well:

> The world is too complicated in all its parts and interconnections to be due to chance alone. I am convinced that the existence of life with all its order in each of its organisms is simply too well put together. Each part of a living thing depends on all its other parts to function. How does each part know? How is each part specified at conception? The more one learns of bio-chemistry the more unbelievable it becomes unless there is some type of organizing principle....[23]

Evidence of intelligence behind living things is not limited to the cosmic or microscopic genetic level. It can be observed with the naked eye. As Louis Agassiz, one of the nineteenth-century pioneers of American biology, observed,

> [Darwin] has lost sight of the most striking of the features, and the one which pervades the whole, namely, that there runs throughout Nature unmistakable evidence of thought, corresponding to the mental operations of our own mind, and therefore intelligible to us as thinking beings, and unaccountable on any other basis than that they own their existence to the working of intelligence; and no theory that overlooks this element can be true to nature.[24]

Nature manifests some amazing designs that are like things known to have intelligent causes. The human eye is an incredible camera which human inventors have not yet rivaled. A bird's wing is amazingly adapted to flight and would have to be completely and wholly intact before flight was possible. Furthermore, nature's anticipatory design bespeaks intelligent forethought. Bodily glands anticipate danger and secrete appropriate chemicals in the blood to enable one to react. Many animals lay their eggs where food and survival are possible for their offspring. All of this resembles an advance plan of some mind beyond creatures that has preprogrammed their "instincts" for the ongoing pattern of life. Even the casual observer cannot avoid seeing the similarities between the kinds of effects known to be produced by intelligent causes and those present in living things.

Of course, some have suggested that this could have happened by purely natural processes apart from an intelligent intervention. Natural selection is often suggested as one such mechanism that makes this possible. However, this response will not suffice when speaking of the origin of the first living organism or first life, for there was no natural selection on the prebiotic level. Natural selection is a process that operates only after life has begun. The evolutionist Theodosius Dobzhansky declared that "prebiotic natural selection is a contradiction in terms."[25]

Some naturalists have speculated that the first living organism could have been more simple than one-cell organisms alive today. But this response is insufficient to negate the argument for an intelligent cause of first life for two reasons. First, it is purely speculative, without any basis in fact. Second, even if the first living organism were more simple, it would still have specified complexity, and that appears to require an intelligent cause. For example, even if the first living thing did not have as much information as an encyclopedia but only as much as one essay in it, it would still need an intelligent cause. Only intelligent beings write articles, or even paragraphs. If an agnostic, like Sagan, would accept a "single message" as proof for supernormal intelligence, then why not the highly complex message known to be in a living cell?

Another bit of evidence for an intelligent Creator of life is the anthropic principle. According to this principle, the universe from its very inception was amazingly well-tuned for the emergence of human life. From the beginning of the cosmos, to the formation of the earth, to the emergence of living things, all conditions were adapted to the eventual appearance of human life. Commenting on these phenomena, one agnostic scientist confessed:

> The anthropic principle is the most interesting development next to the proof of the creation, and it is even more interesting because it seems to say that science itself has proven, as a hard fact, that this universe was made, was designed, for man to live in. It's a very theistic result.[26]

The Origin of Man

The Christian View. Christians differ as to the amount of change that may have been involved in the emergence of new life forms, including human beings. Some, as does this author, allow for only microevolution or variation within created forms. This view is generally called special creation.[27] Others believe that macroevolution may have ocurred between major types of life but only through a divinely directed process of evolution.[28] This view has generally been called "theistic evolution."

Theistic evolutionists point to a progressive series of

fossils from the more simple to the more complex as evidence for such evolution. However, the same data can be explained as the result of a common Creator and not a common ancestor. Study the illustration of this point on the following page.

Notice that the utensils, pots, and pans in this illustration were created by an intelligent human mind for the common purpose of cooking—from the simple measuring spoon to the large cooking pot. Yet this relationship does not at all mean that they were derived from each other; to the contrary, what they share is a common originator, not a common ancestor. Just so it is entirely plausible that the relationship between the more simple and the more complex fossils on record does not indicate progressive development through a common ancestor, but an intelligent and purposeful Creator who created each new life form directly.

Notwithstanding, orthodox Christians have been united in believing that the first human beings did not appear as such apart from a direct creative act of God.

Even though Augustine allowed for long periods of time before humans first appeared in the world,[29] nevertheless he believed God created both man's soul and body. "Though God formed man of the dust of the earth, yet the earth itself, and every earthly material, is absolutely created out of nothing; and man's soul, too, God created out of nothing, and joined to the body, when He made man."[30] Augustine believed that humans are unique creations of God distinct from animals. He declared: "Surely man comes close to God by that part of him which transcends those lower faculties which he has in common even with the beast."[31]

Aquinas too believed that "the life of man, as being the most perfect grade, is not said to be produced, like the life of other animals, by the earth or water, but immediately by

God." Further, he pointed out: "Animals and plants may be said to be produced according to their kinds, to signify their remoteness from the divine image and likeness, whereas man is said to be made in the image and likeness of God."[32] The Protestant reformers, Luther and Calvin, also believed in the direct and special creation of man in God's image and likeness. The Catholic church has continued to maintain that man as a rational being is a special creation of God, however the human physical body came into existence.[33]

Human beings are not simply higher animals but a unique creation in God's image. That has always been the position of the Christian faith down through the ages.

One of the features of human beings that most clearly separates them from lower animals is language. Human language is a product of human reason, and the rational does not emerge from the nonrational any more than being is caused by nonbeing. Human language is distinctive evidence of human creation by a rational Creator.

Human Language Is Unique. No animals speak it or can learn it with true conceptual understanding. Human language differs from animal communication in many ways.[34] For example, it uses abstract symbolism, is independent of stimulus, and is culturally rather than biologically transmitted. Experiments in which animals have learned to imitate human language have failed to teach them these essential qualities. Listen to the words of a scientist who worked on the unsuccessful project to teach a chimpanzee how to speak a human language:

> Despite the frustrations of Project Nim, I knew that there could be no substitute for that intelligent bundle of playfulness and mischief, a creature more human than any

other nonhuman I knew. One of the reasons this parting was so painful was that *there was no way to talk with him about it.* Nim and I were able to sign about simple events in his world and mine. But how could I explain why I and the other project members who came along to Oklahoma suddenly abandoned him? How could we explain that it was necessary to leave him forever in a totally new environment, with a totally new group of human and nonhuman primates?[35]

Another scientist, who once believed chimps could learn to talk our language, eventually discarded his belief in the face of the experimental evidence: "Chimps do not have any significant degree of human language and when, in two to five years, this fact becomes properly disseminated, it will be of interest to ask, Why were we so easily duped by the claim that they do?"[36]

The Human Brain. A powerful argument for the creation of human beings comes from the genetic information in the human brain. Carl Sagan has observed that:

The information content of the human brain expressed in bits is probably comparable to the total number of connections among the neurons—about a hundred trillion bits. If written out in English, say, that information would fill some twenty million volumes, as many as in the world's largest libraries, the equivalent of twenty million books is inside the heads of every one of us. The brain is a very big place in a very small space. . . . The neurochemistry of the brain is astonishingly busy, the circuitry of a machine more wonderful than any devised by humans.[37]

If a single message from space proves an intelligent creator—which is Sagan's view—how about 20 million volumes full of information? If ordinary machines need an intelligent cause, then how about one more wonderful than any devised by humans?

Natural Selection. Of course, noncreationists often point to natural selection as a means by which simple information (life) can evolve into more complex information (life forms). This, however, is a highly dubious alternative to the intervention of an intelligent Creator for two reasons. First, natural selection does not really produce new (higher) forms of life. Natural selection is a survival principle—the survival of the fittest. It does not create new forms but only helps preserve old ones.[38] It can account for the differential survival of variations but not for the variations themselves. It is a survival not an arrival principle.

It is argued by some evolutionists that if artificial selection can produce significant changes in a certain amount of time, then natural selection can produce even greater changes over long periods of time. But this assumes that there is a significant similarity between artificial selection and natural selection. On the contrary, there is a significant difference between them at every major point.[39] For example, artificial selection (AS) has an aim in view, but natural selection (NS) does not. Further AS is an intelligently guided process, but NS is not. Also, in AS there are intelligent choices of breeds, which are then protected from destructive processes, whereas neither is true of NS. In addition, AS preserves desired freaks while NS eliminates most of their freaks. Finally, AS continually interrupts the process to reach its goal, but NS does not. Thus AS has preferential survival as opposed to NS. So rather than being similar, artificial selection and natural selection are in most crucial aspects exactly opposite each other. In order for natural selection to work in the same way as artificial selection, it would have to have an intelligence guiding it somehow. Therefore, this analogy requires some kind of intelligent Creator.

Natural selection fails as a purely natural process because it lacks intelligence to do what can be done by artificial (i.e., intelligent) selection. The only way natural selection can be made to work is to endow it with intelligent powers which atheistic or agnostic evolutionists often (perhaps unwittingly) do. For example, evolutionists of this ilk often say things like the following about natural selection: "It 'designed' our survival";[40] or "It 'arranged' for the continuance of life."[41]

To claim that natural selection can "design" or "arrange," is to say that it has the power of intelligence. In fact, some naturalistic evolutionists endow natural selection not only with the powers of intelligence but also with the power of deity. Charles Darwin himself referred to it as "My deity Natural Selection."[42] The co-inventor of natural selection with Charles Darwin, Alfred Wallace, said natural selection is "a Mind not only adequate to direct and regulate all the forces at work in living organisms, but also the more fundamental forces of the whole material universe."[43]

Conclusion

To sum up, in order to avoid an intelligent Creator of human life, naturalistic evolution postulates natural selection as a "supreme," intelligent "deity" that "guides" the process of evolution toward its eventual "goal" of producing life. In fact, by attempting to avoid an intelligent cause, they substitute one of their own. Not worshiping the Lord and God of all, they create, if unwittingly, a god that supports their cosmology.

Thus, in these crucial ways the present scientific evidence supports the reality of creation as presented in the Bible. Since science is limited and progressive, we should not expect complete agreement in every detail with the biblical presentation. However, the amount of present agreement is striking. It strongly supports the biblical teaching that God created the universe (Gn 1:1), every living thing (1:21), and human beings in his image (1:27). The footprints are there in the sand for all to see.

Part Three

The Moral and Spiritual Implications of Creation

SEVEN

Respect for Creation

W HAT DIFFERENCE DOES IT MAKE whether the world and mankind were created or not? Interestingly enough, both atheist and theist often see similar implications of belief or disbelief in a Creator. In brief, if human life has a divine likeness, then life is sacred. If humans are created in God's likeness then there is a moral obligation to treat them as godlike creatures. If there is a Creator, then the creature has a moral obligation to him. If, on the other hand, humans are just animals that evolved by purely natural processes, then there is no intrinsic reason they should show such ultimate respect. Further, if there is no Creator, then humans are on their own to do as they see fit. Much of the current clash over Judeo-Christian values and secular humanist values springs out of this difference of views on man's origin.

The Vital Relationship between
Our Origins and Our Moral Obligations

There is unexpected agreement between many atheists (and agnostics) and theists over the relationship between where we came from and what we ought to do, between our origins and our obligations. How we got here seems to lead naturally to a consideration of how we ought to behave now that we are here. Ethical questions flow naturally from a discussion of where we come from and therefore who we are.

While Carl Sagan's system does not include God, he does affirm that we have a duty to our point of origin. According to Sagan, "The Cosmos is all that is or ever was or ever will be."[1] In fact, he believes that humans are created in the image of the cosmos. Everything in the universe employs the same patterns over and over again, conservatively and ingenuously.[2] This is true of plants and animals, of oak trees and humans.

Since humans are created in the image of the cosmos, they have a moral obligation to their Creator. "Our obligation to survive is owed not just to ourselves but also to that Cosmos, ancient and vast, from which we spring."[3] In other words, since we have received our existence from the cosmos, we have a duty to perpetuate its existence. Indeed, the very key to our survival is the cosmos on which we float like a speck of dust in a beam of light.[4] So Sagan claims, "It is clear to us that the present and future well being of mankind depends upon scientific knowledge."[5] An openness to the cosmos is necessary to advance our knowledge.[6]

Since Sagan believes we have evolved, he reasons that life must have evolved elsewhere in the universe. Every star may be a sun to someone.[7] Contact with these extraterrestrials could be the salvation of the human race. Hence, we must tune in to outer space (by way of radiotelescopes) to receive a possible message from extraterrestrials. For "the receipt of a single message from space would show that it is possible to live through such technological adolescence."[8] After all, the transmitting civilization has survived. Sagan believes that such knowledge might be worth a great deal; such a message might strengthen the bonds that join all beings on this planet. Since the cosmos is our creator and may be our savior, we have a moral duty to it. Thus scientists (particularly astronomers) are "priests" who remind us of our ethical obligations and show us the way of cosmic salvation.

Another nontheistic thinker who sought both a creator and a savior apart from God was the German philosopher Fredrich Nietzsche. At the very dawn of the twentieth century, Nietzsche saw clearly the relationship between atheism and ethics. He declared that "God is dead. God remains dead. And we have killed him. How shall we, the murderers of all murderers, comfort ourselves?"[9] What shall we then do? Nietzsche answers: "Must not we ourselves become gods simply to seem worthy of it? There has never been a greater deed; and whoever will be born after us—for the sake of this deed he will be part of a higher history than history hitherto."[10] For when God died, all absolutes died with him. There is no moral lawgiver to prescribe right and wrong; we must create our morality. Values do not originate in heaven. We must make them on earth. Thus Nietzsche exhorted his followers:

> I beseech you, my brothers, remain faithful to the earth, and do not believe those who speak to you of other worldly hopes! . . . Once the sin against God was the greatest sin; but God died, and these sinners died with Him. To sin against the earth is now the most dreadful thing. . . ."[11]

In short, if humans were not created by God, then they have no moral duty to him. There are no absolute values to discover; there are only relative values to create. As the great Russian novelist Fyodor Dostoevsky said, if God does not exist, then everything is permitted.

Few atheists have seen the relationship between our origins and our obligations better than the French philosopher Jean-Paul Sartre. For him, God was an impossible concept, a self-caused being. Since there is no God to determine us, we are free, radically and absurdly free. Thus he wrote:

> No sooner had you [Zeus] created me than I ceased to be yours. I was like a man who's lost his shadow. And there was nothing left in heaven, no right or wrong, nor anyone to give me orders. . . .
> I shall not return under your law; I am doomed to have no other law but mine. . . . For I, Zeus, am a man and every man must find his own way.[12]

That is the consequence of being without an ultimate Creator, without God-given values. Sartre answered, "All human activities are equivalent. . . . Thus it amounts to the same thing whether one gets drunk alone or is a leader of nations." Consequently, ethics must begin in despair. In Sartre's words, we must "repudiate the spirit of seriousness" that believes in "transcendent" values.[13] This does not mean there are no values but simply that there are no objective or ultimate ones. Values are not there to be discovered; rather, they are left to be determined by us. The end result of this view of life is a philosophy stripped of any real grounding in the supernatural, a philosophy that relegates God to the ash heap of history.

The End Result of Denying the Creator

In 1933 and 1973, two manifestos were produced affirming such a philosophy of life called humanism. They articulate well the connection between this view of man's origin and his moral obligation. These humanists declared that:

First: religious humanists regard the universe as self-existing and not created.
Second: humanism believes that man is a part of nature and that he has emerged as the result of a continuous process.[14]

Since there is no God and humans evolved by natural processes, secular humanists believe that "the nature of the universe depicted by modern science makes unacceptable any supernatural or cosmic guarantees of human value."[15]

When their manifesto was updated in 1973, they re-affirmed: "Humanists still believe that traditional theism, especially faith in the prayer-hearing God, assumed to love and care for persons, to hear and understand their prayers, and to be able to do something about them, is an unproved and outmoded faith."[16] They affirm further: "As non-theists, we begin with humans not God, nature not deity." Thus, they conclude, "No deity will save us; we must save ourselves."[17]

Secular humanists see clearly that if there is no God, then there can be no moral absolutes. So they conclude: "Moral values derive their source from human experience. Ethics is autonomous and situational, needing no theological or ideological sanction. Ethics stems from human need and interest."[18] Spelled out in particular this means that secular humanists accept "the right to birth control, abortion, . . . divorce, [and any] . . . sexual behavior between consenting adults."[19] In addition to abortion, secular humanists believe in "euthanasia, and the right to suicide." Since there is no

God to be sovereign over life, man is in charge of his own destiny. Humans are in control of "developing the values and goals that determine their lives." Thus secular humanists reject any God-given "decalogues, rules, proscriptions, or regulations."[20]

In brief, the connection between our origins and our obligations is chillingly clear. We have a moral obligation to who or whatever created us. Since atheists do not believe in God, they find their duty is to the cosmos or to nature or to the evolutionary process. If humans are the highest product of naturalistic evolution, then they are in charge. They create their own heaven and hell. They recreate God in their own image. The creature is worshiped instead of the Creator.

Why Christians Spell Creator with a Capital C

Theists agree with atheists that our moral duty is to our Creator, but we spell Creator with a capital C. Genesis tells us that "God created man in his own image" (1:27) and then immediately commanded our first parents: "Be fruitful and multiply, and fill the earth and subdue it" (1:28). God created a paradise for Adam and Eve in which to live (Gn 2:8-9). And then "the Lord God commanded the man, saying, 'You may freely eat of every tree of the garden; but of the tree of the knowledge of good and evil you shall not eat, for in the day that you eat of it you shall die'" (2:16-17).

This same connection between origin and obligation is seen in the Ten Commandments that begin: "I am the Lord your God" (Ex 20:2), and then proceed to command: "You shall have no other gods before me ... you shall not kill. You shall not commit adultery," etc. (Ex 20:3, 13, 14). In other words, the God who made us has a moral right to say to us, "Be holy, for I am holy" (Lv 11:44). He has created us; and he will decide our destiny, not we ourselves.

The Old Testament prophets were very clear about the connection between our creation by God and our subsequent obligation to him. For example, the biblical view sees the relation of the sexes as part of God's original plan of creation. Malachi wrote: "Has not one God created us? Why then are we faithless to one another, profaning the covenant of our fathers?" (Mal 2:10). He then goes on to draw moral implications for marriage declaring: "The Lord was witness to the covenant between you and the wife of your youth" (v. 14). Then Malachi shows the plain connection between our origin in God and our obligation to him, proclaiming,

> Has not the one God made and sustained for us the spirit of life? And what does he desire? Godly offspring. So take heed to yourselves, and let none be faithless to the wife of his youth. "For I hate divorce," says the Lord the God of Israel. (v. 15-16)

Our Moral Obligations to Important Institutions in Society. The Bible draws a direct relationship between the creation of Adam, and then Eve from Adam. Several important institutions are ordered according to this important reality of headship and subordination in human relationships. These institutions include marriage, the home, the church, and human government as understood by God's original purposes in creation.

The key principle to understand God's intention here—as stated briefly in chapter one—is the need for the right ordering of relationships within human community for the sake of unity of mind and heart. It is an order that is reflected in the divine community of the Triune Godhead where, for instance, the Son willingly submitted to the Father in all things for the sake of man's salvation. Without this grounding according to God's original purposes, the important institutions of marriage, the home, the church, and government become seriously undermined—as is the sad case in much of modern society.

Let us turn then to the Bible and briefly consider God's original intentions for these institutions, so we can see afresh our moral obligations as Christians joined together in governing and ordering these vital institutions:

1. The very creation of man and woman forms the basis for marriage. Jesus tells us:

> "Have you not read that he who made them from the beginning made them male and female, and said, 'For this reason a man shall leave his father and mother and be joined to his wife, and the two shall become one flesh?' So they are no longer two but one flesh. What therefore God has joined together, let not man put asunder." (Mt 19:4-6)

We see that the basic reason why divorce is wrong is the creation of man and woman and their subsequent union by God. The New Testament simply does not allow us to disregard the created order and our commitment to such serious moral obligations as the covenant relationship of marriage.

2. Likewise, for this lifelong commitment of marriage to achieve unity of mind and heart, God calls for the exercise of the husband's headship in the home:

> But I want you to understand that the head of every man is Christ, the head of a woman is her husband, and the head of Christ is God.... (For man was not made from woman,

but woman from man. Neither was man created for woman, but woman for man.) (1 Cor 11:3, 8, 9)

Paul is telling us that God's purpose in the home is a complementarity of roles between husband and wife that reflects God's right order and fosters unity. Man is the head of his wife and is himself under submission to Christ. The wife's place is that of a helpmate alongside her husband, submitting to his direction as head of the home, just as he subordinates his will to that of Christ.

3. In turn, understanding this order of creation is the ground for male authority in the church. Just as a husband is head of his wife, so Christ is the head of the church, which is his bride. Standing in Christ's stead, men are meant to exercise the overall shepherding and governing authority in the church. For instance, Paul draws out some of the implications of this when he writes: "Let a woman learn in silence with all submissiveness. I permit no woman to teach or to have authority over men; she is to keep silent. For Adam was formed first, then Eve . . ." (1 Tm 2:11-13). In God's plan for the new creation in Christ, men are called to exercise headship in the home and in the church lovingly and faithfully.

4. Just as there is subordination and headship in marriage, the home, and the church for the sake of unity in Christ, so authority needs to be exercised by human governments to safeguard and protect the dignity of human persons in wider society. And, once again, we see that this institution and its purpose in society is grounded in the fact of creation. As the Lord God said to Noah and his sons after the flood:

For your lifeblood I will surely require a reckoning; of every beast I will require it and of man; of every man's brother I will require the life of man. Whoever sheds the blood of man, by man shall his blood be shed; for God made man in his own image. (Gn 9:5-6)

It is precisely because man is made in God's image and likeness that governments should protect the dignity and rights of the individual human person.

The Relationship between Creation and Other Christian Doctrines. Further, creation is integrally linked to other essential doctrines of the faith. For instance, Adam's creation and fall are directly connected to original sin and God's subsequent plan of salvation:

Therefore as sin came into the world through one man and death through sin, and so death spread to all men because all men sinned . . . If, because of one man's trespass, death reigned through that one man, much more will those who receive the abundance of grace and the free gift of righteousness reign in life through the one man Jesus Christ. (Rom 5:12, 17)

So, too, there is also a clear connection between creation and the resurrection of Christ and all believers:

Thus it is written, "The first man Adam became a living being"; the last Adam [Christ] became a life-giving spirit. But it is not the spiritual which is first but the physical, and then the spiritual. The first man was from the earth, a man of dust; the second man is from heaven. As was the man of dust, so are those who are of dust; and as is the man of heaven, so are those who are of heaven. (1 Cor 15:45-48)

Paul here is contrasting the first man Adam with the last Adam, Christ. The image of "the man of heaven" who "became a lifegiving spirit" clearly refers to the resurrected Christ. And just as the man of heaven was raised from the dead, so will Christian believers—"those who are of heaven"—be raised from the dead. This is the promise of the "New Adam" of the new creation, our Lord Jesus Christ.

Not only that, we have a firm promise that this New Adam will come again to usher in the new creation with a purifying fire of judgment and destruction at the end of time. The old order of creation will pass away:

> First of all, you must understand this, that scoffers will come in the last days with scoffing, following their own passions and saying, "Where is the promise of his coming? For ever since the fathers fell asleep, all things have continued as they were from the beginning of creation. They deliberately ignore this fact, that by the Word of God heavens existed long ago, and an earth formed out of water and by means of water, through which the world that then existed was deluged with water and perished. But by the same word the heavens and earth that now exist have been stored up for fire, being kept until the day of judgment and destruction of ungodly men. (2 Pt 3:3-7)

We see, then, that we can draw important relationships between the creation and other doctrines of the faith. In a very real sense, these relationships and all of the moral obligations discussed point to God's clear directive that we need to respect the order and the purposes of the creation. In particular we need to respect the dignity of our fellow man, who is created in God's image.

The Fundamental Dignity of Man. The reality of creation is the very basis for the dignity of man in both testaments. Moses said that killing humans was wrong because: "God made man in his own image" (Gn 9:6). James added that cursing other humans is wrong for the same reason, pointing to the inconsistent use of our tongues when "with it we bless the Lord and Father, and with it we curse men, who are made in the likeness of God" (Jas 3:9).

Both atheist and theist believe that humans are the highest order of life in this world but for different reasons. Atheists believe this high position comes as a result of a blind naturalistic process of evolution. Theists believe that an intelligent supernatural being created humans in his own image. It is for this reason that theists can be called true humanists.[21] Unless one believes there is an ultimate moral law (which can come only from an ultimate moral law giver), then there is no basis for treating humans with ultimate respect. Of course, one can hold to human values without believing in God, but he cannot justify his belief that humans deserve this high respect without there being a God.

Moreover, according to atheism, man differs from animals only in degree not in kind. Thus man is really only an animal. In theism man is a special creation, different in kind from all animals. It is because of the special nature of their creation that humans deserve the special status that secular humanists desire to accord them. But secular humanists have no justification for claiming such special treatment of mankind if we are only animals. In short, only in the Judeo-Christian concept of the special creation of humans is there a real basis for true humanism. That is, only in a Judeo-Christian view of man as specially created in

God's image and likeness is there a basis for true human freedom, dignity, and moral responsibility.

Many scholars have distinguished between the "image" and "likeness" of God.[22] Others see these words (Gn 1:26) as only a linguistic parallel. Whatever the case, there are at least two aspects to the similarity humans have with God. Humans both represent (image) and resemble (likeness) God. They represent God spiritually and resemble him morally. Because human beings are God's representatives, it is wrong to murder them. For taking another innocent human life is killing God in effigy (Gn 9:6). Because humans resemble God it is wrong to curse them for thereby God is cursed indirectly (Jas 3:9).

The Scriptures are emphatic about treating God's human regents with respect. Jesus said, "As you did it to one of the least of these my brethren, you did it to me" (Mt 25:40). John declared, "He who does not love his brother whom he has seen, cannot love God whom he has not seen" (1 Jn 4:20). For if we do not love humans made in God's image, how can we love the God in whose image they are made?

Jesus summed up the law in two commands: "You shall love the Lord your God with all your heart . . ." and "You shall love your neighbor as yourself" (Mt 22:37, 39). On these two, he said, "depend all the law and prophets" (v. 40). These commandments sum up the moral law: the first describing our duty to God; and the second, our duty to human beings. The first is our vertical responsibility; the second is our horizontal duty.

Since God is supreme, we owe our ultimate allegiance to him. He must be loved with all our heart, mind, and soul. Other human beings are to be loved as ourselves (Mt 22:39). And since "no man ever hates his own flesh, but nourishes and cherishes it" (Eph 5:29), this command is a big order. Love for God is over and above all other objects of love. He is ultimate, and as such deserves no less than our ultimate commitment. He is our Creator, and as creatures, we owe everything to him, even our very being.

Keepers of the Earth

When God created Adam, he gave Adam care over creation, saying, "Fill the earth and subdue it; and have dominion over the fish of the sea and over the birds of the air and over every living thing that moves upon the earth" (Gn 1:28). God "took the man and put him in the garden of Eden to till it and keep it" (Gn 2:15). Not only were humans to be keepers of the earth but they were also to be their "brother's keeper" (Gn 4:9). Thus his duty extended both to the environment that supported human life and to the human life supported by that environment.

The psalmist said, "The earth is the Lord's and the fulness thereof, the world and those who dwell therein" (Ps 24:1). The world is God's garden; mankind are his gardeners. The earth is the Lord's; we are his earth-keepers. How we treat the environment is not an amoral issue. We have a moral obligation under God to be good stewards of the resources that he has entrusted to us. Whatever the area, as the apostle Paul said, "It is required in stewards that a man be found faithful" (1 Cor 4:2, KJV). Mankind was given the duty of dominion (Gn 1:28), but not the right of destruction. We are to cultivate the environment, not corrupt it. We are to plow it, but not pollute it.

It is clear from Scripture that God cares for his creation, and that he requires humans to cooperate in caring for it.

Notice how the psalmist states this divine-human cooperation:

> Thou dost cause the grass to grow for the cattle, and plants for man to cultivate, that he may bring forth food from the earth. . . . The trees of the Lord are watered abundantly, the cedars of Lebanon which he planted. . . . Man goes forth to his work and to his labor until the evening. (Ps 104:14, 16, 23)

God causes the plants to grow, but man is to cultivate them. God created Eden, but Adam was to care for it. Disregard for the Christian view of creation leads to both misunderstanding and misuse of nature.[23] As C.S. Lewis put it, "What we call Man's power over Nature turns out to be a power exercised by some men over other men with Nature as its instrument."[24]

Francis of Assisi, in his famous "Canticle of Brother Sun," articulated beautifully the Christian attitude of respect for God's creation when he wrote:

> All praise be yours, my Lord, through all that you have made,
> And first my lord Brother Sun,
> Who brings the day; and light you give to us through him. . . .
> All praise be yours, my Lord, through Brothers Wind and Air,
> And fair and stormy, all the weather's moods,
> By which you cherish all that you have made.
> All praise be yours, my Lord, through Sister Water,
> So useful, lowly, precious and pure.[25]

The creation reveals the Creator (Ps 19:1; Rom 1:20). Hence, to pollute the world is to mar the mirror that reflects its maker. Destruction of the environment distorts its ability to convey the Creator.

Admittedly, not all Christians have lived up to these elementary duties of stewardship. There is a strange irony about man's relation to his environment. If people pollute their environment, they have destroyed its ability to preserve them. Humans were made to be the earth's keepers. But if they do not keep the earth, then the earth will not keep them. The question men should ask themselves today is this: "*Am I my earth's keeper?*" For if I am not the earth's keeper, then it is becoming increasingly evident that neither am I my brother's keeper. For this is my brother's earth. And if I do not keep it, then it will keep neither him nor me.

Absolute Respect for Human Life

While the physical universe manifests God's glory, only humans are said to be made in his image and likeness. This is man's fundamental dignity, as we have already seen. Hence, respect for human beings is given special place in God's economy. This is why one of the Ten Commandments explicitly exhorted, "You shall not murder" (Ex 20:13, NIV). Respect for human life from beginning to end is a top priority in our ethical responsibility to God's creation.

It matters not whether the person is very young or very old; they are still human. It makes no difference whether they are seen as important or inconsequential in the eyes of the world, whether they are conscious or unconscious, whether they are intelligent or retarded. None of these accidental conditions are essential characteristics of being human. Killing innocent humans is never justified as such whatever the circumstances.

God alone is sovereign over life. "The Lord gives and the Lord takes away" (Jb 1:21; Dt 32:39). The Christian approach toward the dying should be one of mercy, not murder. We can help kill the pain but should not kill the person, for he or she is sacred in God's eyes. We should shoot the patient with a sedative but not with a bullet. The Bible says, "Give strong drink to him who is perishing, and wine to those in bitter distress" (Prv 31:6).

The logical implication of humans being created in God's image is the duty of protecting human life from conception to death. Likewise, the logical conclusion of the alternative view is the freedom to destroy all undesirable human life.

Hitler accepted Darwin's evolutionary principle of "survival of the fittest" and applied it to the races. For him, the highest good was not God, but human nature, realized in the Aryan race. He reasoned that it was our obligation to continue evolution by eliminating the races he considered inferior, such as the Jews. He concluded that:

> In order to preserve a certain culture, the type of manhood that creates such a culture must be preserved. But such a preservation goes hand-in-hand with the inexorable law that it is the strongest and the best who must triumph and that they have the right to endure. He who would live must fight. He who does not wish to fight in this world, where permanent struggle is the law of life, has not the right to exist.[26]

With that Hitler killed some twelve million human beings, six million of whom were Jews. Without God, he created his own hell and determined who went there. And he created his own warped version of heaven in the guise of racial supremacy and superiority.

Secular humanists insist there is no God. Humans, therefore, are not created in his image. Mankind then is in charge of making its own rules. Man decides who lives and who dies. This applies to both before and after birth. This chilling doctrine comes from the same source and has much the same effect as Hitler's genocide, although secular humanists do not state their case as boldly.

One secular philosopher, Mary Anne Warren, testified before a presidential commission on biomedical ethics (1982) that a severely disabled newborn baby was like a horse with a broken leg that needed to be killed. This, she claimed, would spare the baby from the agony of a slow and painful death.[27] Here the naturalistic evolutionary view that we are only animals becomes more explicit in the comparison. The baby is seen as a poor thing to be put out of its misery the way we would a hopelessly injured household pet.

Where do we end up with this kind of devaluation of human life? Consider this example. After conducting experiments on babies aborted by hysterotomy in which he sliced open the stomachs and cut off the heads of live babies, Dr. Marti Kekomaki justified his experiments saying, "An aborted baby is just garbage and that's where it ends up."[28]

Some abortionists have been very explicit in their comparison of humans with animals. Professor Peter Singer, an advocate of abortion, has even argued that "the life of a fetus is of no greater value than the life of a nonhuman animal...." He adds that "it must be admitted that these arguments apply to the newborn baby as much as to the fetus." So "the life of a newborn baby is of less value than the life of a pig, a dog, or a chimpanzee."[29] Such is the disregard for human life that results from the denial that human beings are created in God's image.

The last two centuries can be succinctly summarized as follows: in the nineteenth century God died; in the twentieth century man died. More precisely, man killed God in the nineteenth century, and man is killing man in the twentieth century.

The logic seems inevitable: when God is denied in whose image humans are made, then humans are denied as made in the image of God. The dignity of the creature is based in the reality of God's creation. Likewise, without the recognition of man's divine *origin*, there is no basis for divine *obligations*. Human responsibility follows from the reality of creation. Without that recognition, a Hitler or a Stalin has a free hand to do what he may.

EIGHT

Reverence for the Creator

E VEN NONTHEISTS ACKNOWLEDGE A RELATIONSHIP between
the origin of all things and reverence or awe, between
what theists call creation and adoration. Frederich
Schleiermacher, the father of liberal Protestant theology,
had a sense of "absolute dependence" on the universe from
which he sprang. For he confessed "a sense of man's
insignificance and impotence in the face of the universe...."[1] The atheist Sigmund Freud admitted having the
same feelings.[2] Julian Huxley, a celebrated agnostic, spoke
of moments of "spiritual refreshment" from seeing a
beautiful landscape.[3]

Many nontheists have even personified or deified the
causes they believed in. In a frank moment Charles Darwin
said:

> To believe in miraculous creations or in the "continued
> intervention of creative power" . . . is to make "my deity
> 'Natural Selection' superfluous" and to hold *the* Deity—if
> such there be—accountable for phenomena which are
> rightly attributed only to his magnificent laws.[4]

Darwin defended his use of the phrase "my deity Natural
Selection," saying, "I speak of natural selection as an active

power or deity; but who objects to an author speaking of the attraction of gravity as ruling the movements of the planets." He adds, "It is difficult to avoid personifying nature."[5]

Evolutionary philosopher Herbert Spencer spoke of cosmic evolution as the "manifestations of this infinite and eternal power."[6] The German evolutionist Ernst Haekel boasted that evolution had annulled the infinite Deity and ushered in "a new era of infinite knowledge."[7] Elsewhere he deified nature and spoke in personal terms of "loving" it. For he believed that "the paths which lead to the noble divinity of truth and knowledge are the loving study of nature and its laws."[8]

Perhaps the nontheist who has best stated the connection between the origin of all things and awe, creation and worship, is Carl Sagan. He believes that humans are literally made in the image of the cosmos. Human beings are simply "stardust contemplating stars."[9] For we are "the product of a long series of biological accidents"[10] from molecule to man. For Sagan, "evolution is a fact, not a theory."[11] Human beings have emerged from the cosmos by a powerful random process.[12] Our more immediate origin is the sea. Hence, Sagan writes: "The ocean calls. Some part of our being knows this is from where we came. We long to return. These aspirations are not, I think, irreverent, although they may trouble whatever gods may be."[13]

As we contemplate the "deep mystery" of the universe,[14] a sense of awe arises. For we find "something astonishing."[15] Indeed we see the "marvelous" arrangement of matter.[16] It is something "wonderful" and "awesome."[17] In fact, it even elicits worship from us. The cosmos is our creator. For "the sun warms us and feeds us and permits us to see. It fecundated the Earth. It is powerful beyond human experience. Birds greet the sunrise with an audible ecstasy." Thus Sagan concludes,

> Our ancestors worshiped the Sun, and they were far from foolish. And yet the Sun is an ordinary, even a mediocre star. If we must worship a power greater than ourselves, does it not make sense to revere the Sun and stars?[18]

Sagan believes that we owe admiration to the cosmos for our ancestry. If humans are created in the image of the cosmos, then they owe allegiance to it. Our Creator deserves our worship.

Furthermore, the need for worship is engrained in the heart of the creature. Even atheists demonstrate the need to worship. Carl Sagan suggested we worship the cosmos. Ayn Rand worshiped the human ego. One of her followers said bluntly, "You should worship yourself."[19] Darwin was committed to his "deity Natural Selection." Spencer revered evolution as a cosmic Force. As Paul Tillich noted, everyone has an ultimate. Everyone makes an ultimate commitment to something, whether it is Self, State, Humanity, or the Force. Man is incurably religious. He must worship. If he does not worship the Creator, then he will "worship and serve the creature" (Rom 1:25).

The Harvard atheist Walter Kaufman declared that man is a God-intoxicated ape. The French atheist Albert Camus confessed that "nothing can discourage the appetite for divinity in the heart of man."[20] Likewise his fellow countryman and fellow existentialist Jean-Paul Sartre cried out, "I needed God."[21] Even the German atheist Frederick Nietzsche bemoaned the fact he had no God, saying,

I hold up before myself the images of Dante and Spinoza, who were better at accepting the lot of solitude ... and in the end ... all those who somehow still had a "God" for company. ... My life now consists in the wish that it might be otherwise . . . and that somebody might make my "truths" appear incredible to me.[22]

We see that even atheists stand in awe of what they believe is ultimate, whether it is the universe, the cosmos, or some concept of the all. Although they often deny the word "worship," they consistently bow before gods of their own making. Even secular humanists have an object of their devotion: mankind. Indeed, by their own confession they are religious. In *Humanist Manifesto I*, they described themselves as a "religion" proclaiming, "Humanism is a philosophical, religious, and moral point of view. . . ." They add, "to establish such a religion [of humanism] is a major necessity of the present."[23] An astute observer noted that *Secular Humanism* is one of the major religions of our time, saying,

Humanism is one of the vital religions, perhaps no longer growing but very much alive. It is the dominant religion of our time, a part of the lives of nearly everyone in the "developed" world and of all others who want to participate in a similar development.[24]

As religious people, atheists "worship," that is they attribute ultimate worth to something, whether it is matter or mankind. They evidence the same need to worship as do Christians; they just fulfill it in a different way. Many find fulfillment in the "wonder" of scientific explorations, others in beauty or art. The sense of the sublime (art) is a kindred feeling to the sense of the supreme (religion). Many have confused lace and grace. The bottom line seems to be that humans must worship something; if not the God who made them, then the gods they make.

Theistic Worship

Theists agree with Sagan in principle: the creature should worship his Creator. We dissent only when we are told the cosmos is our Creator. For the cosmos is changing, and God never changes (Mal 3:6; Heb 1:11-12). The cosmos had a beginning, and God is eternal (Ps 90:2). The cosmos is finite, but God is infinite (Ps 147:5). The nontheists are right in acknowledging that we owe awe to our ultimate ancestry. But they are wrong in believing the cosmos is ultimate.

We Do Owe Worship to the Creator. For "being then God's offspring, we ought not think that the Deity is like gold, or silver or stone" (Acts 17:29). God is not constituted of the same stuff as stars. "God is spirit, and those who worship him must worship in spirit and truth" (Jn 4:24). God made man in his own image, but he forbids us making gods in our own image. "You shall not make for yourself a graven image, or any likeness of anything that is in heaven above, or that is in the earth beneath, or that is in the water under the earth" (Ex 20:4). Jesus declared, "You shall worship the Lord your God and him only shall you serve" (Mt 4:10).

Speaking to the Athenian philosophers, Paul declared, "What you worship as unknown, this I proclaim to you. The God who made the world and everything in it. . . ." (Acts 17:23-24). God is not an unknown force, but a known

Father who made and provides for all things. Indeed, "he himself gives to all men life and breath and everything" (Acts 17:25). Everything we have and are as creatures we owe to our Creator. John Calvin observed, for example:

[He] is a jealous God, and will be a stern avenger if he is confounded with any false god; and thereafter defines what due worship is, in order that the human race may be kept in obedience. . . . unless everything peculiar to divinity is confined to God alone, he is robbed of his honour, and his worship is violated.[25]

We Should Reverence the Creator. As Paul reminded the heathen at Lystra, "God gives every good thing in its season." Thus "he has never left himself without a witness" to his gracious provision for his creation (Acts 14). God clothes the lilies and feeds the ravens (Mt 6:26-30). It is because we are totally dependent on our Creator that we owe him worship. Reverence for God is based on our creaturely relationship to God. He is the giver of all things, and we are the receiver of all things. Hence, we should not bite but bless the hand that feeds us. We pray, "Give us this day our daily bread." But every creature is also aware in the depth of his being that: "Man cannot live by bread alone, but by every word that proceeds from the mouth of God" (Mt 4:4). We owe him all, and we owe him awe. He is worthy of all, and we should ascribe all worth to him. Reverence for the Creator is deeply rooted in the reality of creation.

The Nature of Worship

God's Greatness. Recognition of God's greatness is at the heart of worship. God is great, and greatly to be praised.

Thus the psalmist proclaimed,

> All the nations thou hast made shall come
>   and bow down before thee, O Lord,
>   and shall glorify thy name.

Why?

> Thou art great and doest wondrous things,
>   thou alone art God. (Ps 86:9-10)

This same connection between worship and God's greatness is manifest throughout Scripture. "Ascribe to the Lord the glory due his name; bring an offering, and come into his courts" (Ps 96:8). Why? Because "the world is established, it shall never be moved" (v. 10). Even the famous passage on God's holiness in which the angels sang "holy, holy, holy" (Is 6) and extolled the greatness of God is based on worship. For Isaiah saw the Lord "high and lifted up, and his [royal] train filled the temple" (v. 1). Thus it is the greatness of God the Creator, as well as his holiness, that leads Isaiah to cry out "Woe is me! . . . for my eyes have seen the King, the Lord of hosts!" (v. 5). As J.I. Packer aptly noted:

> The angels' song which Isaiah heard in the temple, with its emphatic repetitions—"Holy, holy, holy, is the LORD of hosts" (Is 6:3)—could be used as a motto-text to sum up the theme of the whole Old Testament. The basic idea which the word "holy" expresses is that of separation, or separateness. When God is declared to be "holy," the thought is of all that separates Him and sets Him apart and makes Him different from His creatures.[26]

Psalm 66 states the connection between God's greatness and our worship of him in clear terms:

So great is thy power that thy enemies cringe before thee. All the earth worships thee; they sing praises to thee, sing praises to thy name. (vv. 3-4)

Isaiah 40 is one of the most forceful passages on God's greatness. The prophet exhorted Israel: "Lift up your eyes on high and see: who created these [countless stars]?" (v. 26). The answer: "The Lord is the everlasting God, the Creator of the ends of the earth." He is so great that "he does not faint or grow weary, his understanding is unsearchable" (v. 28). In view of God's greatness as Creator, the prophet responds for the creatures, "They will make supplication to you, saying, 'God is with you only, and there is no other, no god besides him'" (Is 45:14).

Our Response to His Goodness. Worship is not only a recognition of God's greatness, but also a response to his goodness. "Every good endowment and every perfect gift is from above" (Jas 1:17). God gives "every good thing in its season" (Acts 14:17). Whether from God or man, there is only one appropriate response to the reception of good gifts. Shakespeare said, "A thankless son makes a hapless father." This is true in heaven as well as on earth.

The believer is urged: "Give thanks in all circumstances" (1 Thes 5:18). We are to "enter his gates with thanksgiving, and his courts with praise! Give thanks to him, bless his name!" (Ps 100:4). Thus, praise and thanks are linked together. Praise is an essential part of worship. As the psalmist said, "All the earth worships thee; they sing praise to thee, sing praise to thy name" (66:4). Yes, all creation rightly praises the Creator.

Praise. Praise is the response of a grateful heart. It is like the fine mist arising from a waterfall. As God pours out his goodness upon his creatures, they respond in worship that returns to its very source. The creature praises the Creator. Often when Jesus healed the sick they would respond to his goodness by praise. When the crippled woman was immediately made straight by Jesus, "she praised God" (Lk 13:13). When the leper saw that he was healed, he "turned back, praising God with a loud voice, and he fell on his face at Jesus' feet, giving him thanks" (Lk 17:15-16). Likewise, after Jesus restored sight to the blind man, he followed Jesus "glorifying God; and all the people, when they saw it, gave praise to God" (Lk 18:43).

Glory. Within the response of worship to the Creator and Lord of all is not only adoration but also glorification. Glory is manifest excellence. It is an outward manifestation of the inward character of God. John said of Jesus, "The Word became flesh and dwelt among us, full of grace and truth; we have beheld his glory, glory as of the only son from the Father" (Jn 1:14). Glory is to God's essence what a magnifying glass is to a precious jewel: it makes its hidden beauty more manifest. Thus when we glorify God we do not make him more glorious, but we make more evident the goodness of his nature. We read, for example, that when Paul "related one by one the things that God had done among the Gentiles, . . . they glorified God" (Acts 21:19-20).

Supplication and Service. Worship is not only a spiritual but also a practical manifestation of our appreciation to God for his goodness in creating and redeeming us. We should not only praise him for his goodness but also serve him because of it. We should not be mere containers of his goodness but conveyors of it. Service is a way to worship

God, and our service for God will lead others to glorify him. There are two sides to worship: supplication and service. Praise and practice go hand in hand. These two aspects of true worship can be summed up as follows:

Worship	
Supplication	Service
Upward	Outward
Godward	Manward
Praise	Practice
Faith	Works
Thankfulness	Helpfulness
Gratefulness to God	Gifts to others
With our heart	With our hands

The Scriptures often use the word worship as inclusive of service for others. The words "worship" and "serve" are repeatedly used together (1 Kgs 9:6; Rom 1:25; Mt 4:10). The magi worshiped Jesus by giving him gifts of gold, frankincense, and myrrh (Mt 2:11). Likewise, Abraham went to "worship" God on Mt. Moriah by taking Isaac to offer up to God (Gn 22:5). Service and sacrifice are an integral part of our worship of God the Creator. Doing good for his people brings glory to God. Jesus said, "As you did it to one of the least of these my brethren, you did it to me" (Mt 25:40). In point of fact, John reminds us that if we do not love our brother in need we have seen, then we cannot be said really to love God whom we have not seen (1 Jn 4:20).

Our Need to Worship

All creatures need to worship. This is part of the reality of their creation. One can understand why non-believers do not worship the Creator. What is amazing is that many believers do not seem to recognize their need to worship God as Creator. This failure seems to have no denominational prejudice. It is true of both liturgical and non-liturgical churches, of Catholic and Protestant communions. The churches with a more developed liturgy can lose the reality of worship in ritual. The less ritualistic often spend more time in fellowship than worship. They lose the God of their experience in their quest for an experience of God. The focus is more on the gifts than on the giver himself.

True worship of the Creator and Lord of all has become a lost art in the Christian church. The very people who have the greatest need to worship do not sense their great need to worship. Those who confess that God is great and good in the Creeds seldom tell him this from their heart in their confession. We who believe that God has ultimate worth as the Creator of all are so caught up in the immediate that we take very little time telling him about it.

The theological need for worship is based in God's nature as Creator and in our nature as creatures. Creatures have a built-in need to recognize their Creator. As Augustine said, the heart is restless until it finds its rest in God. The creature by nature is not the ultimate itself. It cries out for the source of its life. The creature does not find ultimate satisfaction in anything short of the Creator, regardless of where it looks "under the sun." Solomon tried wine, women, worldliness, wisdom, and works. He concluded, "All was vanity and a striving after wind, and there was nothing to be gained under the sun" (Eccl 2:11). Why? Because God "has put eternity into man's mind" (3:11). A heart with a thirst for the eternal cannot be satisfied with temporal things. There is a God-sized vacuum in the human heart that will not be happy with anything less than God. True happiness is not found "under the sun." It is found only beyond the sun in the one who created the sun, in the Son. "Remember now your Creator," concluded Solomon (12:1). Our very nature as creatures points up to the Creator. We have a deep and ineradicable need to worship.

Why God Seeks Our Worship

God is absolutely perfect and self-contained. By nature God needs nothing: "Nor is he served by human hands, as though he needed anything, since he himself gives to all men life and breath and everything" (Acts 17:25). Why then does he "seek" worshipers (Jn 4:23) and become "jealous" (Ex 20:5) when we worship anyone else? Why does God seem to demand admiration? Is God a cosmic egotist? After much struggle with this question, C.S. Lewis responded with this insightful comparison with a great work of art:

The sense in which the picture "deserves" or "demands" admiration is rather this; that admiration is the correct, adequate or appropriate response to it, that, if paid, admiration will not be "thrown away," and that if we do not admire we shall be stupid, insensible, and great losers, we shall have missed something. In that way many objects both in Nature and in Art may be said to deserve, or merit, or demand admiration.[27]

Lewis then concludes, "It was from this end, which will seem to some irreverent, that I found it best to approach the idea that God 'demands' praise."[28]

In short, God does not need our worship; rather, it is we who need to worship him. God deserves worship, but we benefit from it. It is good for the soul to recognize its supreme end. It is right for creatures to reverence their Creator. With all of creation we need to fall before his throne and join in singing with the saints and angels:

Worthy art thou, our Lord and God, to receive glory and honor and power, for thou didst create all things, and by thy will they existed and were created. (Rv 4:11)

Appendices

Appendix 1

Isaiah 17:7
Isaiah 22:11
Isaiah 27:11
Isaiah 29:16
Isaiah 37:16, 26
Isaiah 40:21, 26, 28
Isaiah 41:20
Isaiah 42:5
Isaiah 43:1, 7, 10, 17, 21
Isaiah 44:2, 21, 24
Isaiah 45:7, 8, 12, 18
Isaiah 48:13
Isaiah 49:5
Isaiah 51:13, 16
Isaiah 54:5, 16
Isaiah 57:16
Isaiah 66:2, 22

Jeremiah 1:5
Jeremiah 10:11-13, 16
Jeremiah 27:5
Jeremiah 29:9
Jeremiah 31:35
Jeremiah 32:17
Jeremiah 33:2
Jeremiah 51:15, 16

Ezekiel 21:30
Ezekiel 28:13, 15

Hosea 8:14

Amos 4:13
Amos 5:8
Amos 9:6

Jonah 1:9

Habakkuk 1:14

Zechariah 12:1

Malachi 2:10, 15

Matthew 13:35
Matthew 19:4, 8

Matthew 24:21
Matthew 25:34

Mark 10:6
Mark 13:19
Mark 16:15

Luke 3:38
Luke 11:50

John 1:3, 10
John 8:44
John 9:32
John 17:5

Acts 7:50
Acts 14:15
Acts 17:24

Romans 1:19-20
Romans 5:14-19
Romans 8:19-23, 39
Romans 9:20

1 Corinthians 11:8, 9, 12
1 Corinthians 15:22, 38, 45-47

2 Corinthians 4:6

Ephesians 1:4
Ephesians 3:9

Colossians 1:16-17, 23
Colossians 3:10

1 Timothy 2:13
1 Timothy 4:3, 4

Hebrews 1:2, 3, 10, 14
Hebrews 3:4
Hebrews 4:3-4, 10, 13
Hebrews 9:11, 26
Hebrews 12:27

1 Peter 1:20
1 Peter 4:19

2 Peter 3:4-7

Revelation 3:14
Revelation 4:8-11
Revelation 10:6
Revelation 13:8
Revelation 14:7
Revelation 17:8
Revelation 21:1, 5
Revelation 22:13

Appendix Two

The Four Basic Views on Creation

There are four basic views on origins (see Geisler, *Origin Science,* 165 f.). Two are naturalistic views and two are supernaturalistic. The naturalistic views are called 1) Naturalistic Creation and 2) Naturalistic Evolution. The supernatural ones are named 3) Theistic Creation and 4) Theistic Evolution. They can be diagrammed as follows:

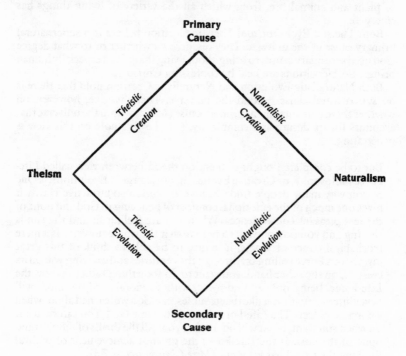

(Geisler, *Origin Science*, p. 166)

1. *Naturalistic Evolution* believes there is no God involved in creation. Things emerged by purely natural processes. Carl Sagan and Isaac Asimov are proponents of this view.

2. *Naturalistic Creation* believes there is no theistic Creator beyond the world but only a creative Mind within the universe that creates. This view is held by Fred Hoyle and N.C. Wickramasinghe.

3. *Theistic Evolution* holds that there is a God beyond the world who created it, but that from that point on all living things emerged under his control by largely natural processes. This position is held by many scholars who confess to be Christian. Most Christians who hold this view would exempt man's soul from this process as a direct creation of God.

4. *Theistic Creation* contends that God directly created the universe, living things, and human beings body and soul. Those in this camp differ on how many things were created and how much time it took God to create them. But there is agreement that God was directly involved in creating the world, life, and mankind. Most believe, as I do, that God directly created different forms of plant and animal life, from which all the variety of living things has emerged.

Both Theistic Evolution and Theistic Creation believe in a supernatural primary cause of the universe. They disagree on whether or to what degree God used secondary causes to bring about living things and especially human beings. Both positions are held by confessing Christians.

Both Naturalistic Evolution and Naturalistic Creation hold that there is no supernatural cause beyond the universe. They disagree, however, on whether there is an intelligent primary cause (Mind) within the universe that accounts for its design and complexity. C.S. Lewis's note on this view is penetrating:

> But to be complete I ought to mention the In-between view called Life-Force philosophy, or Creative Evolution, or Emergent Evolution.... One reason why many people find Creative Evolution so attractive is that it gives one much of the emotional comfort of believing in God and none of the less pleasant consequences. When you are feeling fit and the sun is shining and you do not want to believe that the whole universe is a mere mechanical dance of atoms, it is nice to be able to think of this great mysterious Force rolling on through the centuries and carrying you on its crest. If, on the other hand, you want to do something rather shabby, the Life-Force, being only a blind force, with no morals and no mind, will never interfere with you like that troublesome God we learned about when we were children. The Life-Force is a sort of tame God. You can switch it on when you want, but it will not bother you. All the thrills of religion and none of the cost. Is the Life-Force the greatest achievement of wishful thinking the world has yet seen? (*Mere Christianity*, p. 35)

Chapter Notes

Chapter One
God and Creation

1. *Bara* does not always mean to make something out of nothing (see Gn 2:3; Is 41:20). However, used in the context of the original events of creation described in Genesis 1 it bears this meaning.
2. Giovanni Pettinato, *The Archives of Ebla*, (Garden City, New York: Doubleday & Co., 1981), p. 259.
3. See Norman L. Geisler and Win Corduan, *Philosophy of Religion*, (Grand Rapids, Michigan: Baker Book House, 1988), chapter 9.
4. See Augustine, *Confessions* in *Nicene and Post-Nicene Fathers*, edited by Philip Schaff (Grand Rapids, Michigan: Eerdmans, 1979), vol. 1, chapter 11.
5. Plotinus, *The Enneads*, trans. by Stephen MacKenna (London: Faber and Faber Limited, 1966) 1.8.7.
6. Mary Baker Eddy, *Science and Health with Key to the Scripture*, (Boston: Published by the Trustees under the Will of Mary Baker G. Eddy, 1934), pp. 480-584.
7. G.C. Berkouwer, *Man: The Image of God*, trans. by Dirk W. Jellema (Grand Rapids, Michigan: Eerdmans, 1962), chapter 6.

Chapter Two
Creation: Man and the Cosmos

1. Pierre Simon de Laplace, *The System of the World*, 2 vols. (London: Longman, Rees, Orme, Brown, and Green, 1830) 2:4:331.
2. C.S. Lewis, *Miracles*, (New York: The Macmillan Company, 1947), chapters 14-16.

Chapter Three
Spiritual Creation: The Angels and Heaven

1. Some argue that the "sons of God" in Genesis 6 are angels (cf. Jb 1:6; 2:1; 38:7) who married. But even if angels are involved here, they must have assumed or indwelt some physical bodies on earth. For angels are by nature spirits, and as such "neither marry nor are given in marriage" (Mt 22:30).

2. I have not discussed hell in this chapter as part of spiritual creation because, properly speaking, it was not part of God's desire for creation. Its creation became a necessity after Satan and one-third of the angels in heaven rebelled against God and were cast down into hell, the place God "prepared" as the just punishment for their sin. In a very real sense, then, hell is a distortion or perversion of God's originally good intention for all of his creation. Even now God is patient, "not wishing that any should perish but that all should reach repentance" (2 Pt 3:9).

Chapter Four
The Three Philosophical Views of Creation

1. See Plato, *Timaeus in Collected Dialogues of Plato,* edited by Edith Hamilton and Huntington Cairns (New York: Pantheon Books, 1964), pp. 27ff.
2. See Karl Marx, *Marx and Engels on Religion,* edited by Reinhold Niebuhr (New York: Schocken Books Inc., 1964), p. 298.
3. Carl Sagan, *Cosmos,* (New York: Random House, 1980), p. 4.
4. Karl Marx, ibid., p. 231.
5. Anthony Kenny, *Five Ways: St. Thomas Aquinas' Proofs of God's Existence,* (New York: Schocken Books Inc., 1969), p. 147.
6. Isaac Asimov, *The Beginning of the End,* (New York: Doubleday, 1977), p. 148.
7. Paul Kurtz, *Humanist Manifestos I & II,* (Buffalo, New York: Prometheus Books, 1973), p. 16.
8. Ibid., pp. 16-17.
9. Thomas Hobbes, *Leviathan in Great Books of the Western World,* edited by Robert M. Hutchins (Chicago: Encyclopedia Britannica, 1952), vol. 23, p. 269.
10. Parmenides, *Proem* in G.S. Kirk and J.E. Ravan, *The Presocratic Philosophers,* (Cambridge: University Press, 1964), pp. 266-283.
11. Cited by Swami Prabhavananda, *The Spiritual Heritage of India,* (Hollywood, California: Vedanta Press, 1963), p. 55.
12. Other kinds of pantheism include 1) Emanational (Plotinus), 2) Developmental (Hegel), 3) Modal (Spinoza), 4) Multilevel (Radhakrishnan), and 5) Permeational (Zen Buddhism). See Norman L. Geisler and William Watkins, *Worlds Apart: A Handbook on World Views,* (Grand Rapids, Michigan: Baker Books, 1988), chapter 4.
13. Marilyn Ferguson, *The Aquarian Conspiracy,* (Los Angeles: J.P. Tarcher, Inc., 1980), p. 382.
14. Shirley MacLaine, *Dancing in the Light,* (New York: Bantam Books, 1985), p. 112.
15. From Shirley MacLaine TV special aired in January, 1987.
16. Benjamin Creme, *Messages from Maitreya the Christ,* (Los Angeles: Tara Center, 1980), vol. 1, p. 204.

17. Peter Kreeft, *Between Heaven and Hell,* Downers Grove, Illinois: InterVarsity Press, 1982), p. 92.
18. Augustine, *City of God,* in Schaff, ibid., vol. 2, 11.23.
19. Augustine, *Literal Commentary on Genesis,* trans. by John Hammond Taylor (New York: Newman Press, 1982), p. 23.
20. Augustine, *City of God,* in Schaff, ibid., vol. 2, 11.10.
21. Aquinas, *Summa Theologica,* in *Basic Writings of Saint Thomas Aquinas* (New York: Random House, 1944) 1.46.1. The quotations that follow under this subheading are all drawn from Aquinas' discussion of creation in Part 1, questions 45-46.
22. Augustine, *City of God,* Schaff, ibid., vol. 2, 11.9.
23. Augustine, *Literal Commentary on Genesis,* Taylor, ibid., p. 35.
24. Augustine, *On the Nature of the Good,* in Schaff, ibid., vol. 4, 27.
25. Augustine, *On the Soul and its Origin,* in Schaff, ibid., vol. 5, 1.4.
26. Aquinas, *Summa Theologica* in Pegis, ibid., 1.46.2.
27. Ibid. 1.45.1.
28. Ibid. 1.61.1.
29. Aquinas, *On the Power of God,* trans. by English Dominican Fathers (Westminster, Maryland: Newman Press, 1952) 3.15.
30. Aquinas, *Summa Theologica* in Pegis, ibid., 1.46.2.
31. Aquinas, *Summa Theologica* in Pegis, ibid., 1.46.3.
32. Augustine, *City of God,* in Schaff, ibid., vol. 2, 11.5.
33. Aquinas, *Summa Theologica,* in Pegis, ibid., 1.46.1.
34. Augustine, *Literal Commentary on Genesis,* ibid., p. 195.
35. Augustine, *City of God,* in Schaff, ibid., 11.5.
36. Aquinas, *Summa Theologica,* in Pegis, ibid., 1.46.2.
37. Augustine, *City of God,* in Schaff, ibid., 11.23.
38. Aquinas, *Summa Theologica,* in Pegis, ibid., 1.47.1.
39. Augustine, *City of God,* in Schaff, ibid., 11.3.
40. Ibid., 10.3.
41. Augustine, *Confessions,* in Schaff, ibid., 1.1.

Chapter Five
The Philosophical Arguments for Creation

1. St. Augustine, *On the Creed,* in *Nicene and Post-Nicene Fathers,* edited by Philip Schaff (Grand Rapids, Michigan: Eerdmans, 1979), vol. 3, sect. 4, p. 370.
2. See Aquinas, *Summa Theologica,* in Basic Writings of Thomas Aquinas, Anton C. Pegis ed. (New York: Random House, 1944) 1.2.3.
3. St. Bonaventure, 2 *Sententiarium,* in Etienne Gilson, *The Philosophy of St. Bonaventure* trans. by Dom Illtyd Trethowan and F.J. Sheed (London: Sheed & Ward, 1938), 1.1.1.2.1-6.
4. Aquinas says "to take away the cause is to take away the effect." See *Summa Theologica,* in Pegis, ibid., 1.2.3.
5. See Jonathan Edwards, "Of Being" in *Jonathan Edwards: Representative Selections, with Introductions, Bibliography, and Notes,* by Clarence H.

Faust and Thomas H. Johnson (New York: Hill and Wang, 1962), pp. 18-19.

6. Anselm's first argument went like this:
   1) God is by definition an absolutely perfect being.
   2) Existence is a perfection.
   3) Therefore, God must exist. (If he did not, then he would lack a perfection and not be absolutely perfect.)
   Most thinkers, since Kant, agree with his criticism of Anselm that existence is not a perfection or attribute.

7. St. Anselm, *Proslogium of St. Anselm: Basic Writings,* trans. by S.W. Deane (La Salle, Illinois: Open Court Publishing Company, 1962), 1-6, 15 and *Reply to Gaunilon,* 1-10.

8. See Norman L. Geisler and Win Corduan, *Philosophy of Religion,* (Grand Rapids, Michigan: Baker Book House, 1988), pp. 159-161 and N.L. Geisler, "The Missing Premise in the Ontological Argument" in *Religious Studies* (Sept., 1973) 9.3.

9. William Paley, *Natural Theology,* ed. by Frederick Ferre (New York: Bobbs-Merrill, (1802) (1963), chapter 1.

10. See ibid., chapter 5.

11. David Hume, *Dialogues Concerning Natural Religion,* (New York: Hafner Publishing Company, 1957) Part 8.

12. Sir Fred Hoyle, *Evolution from Space,* (London: Dent, 1981), pp. 24-26.

13. David Hume, *An Inquiry Concerning Human Understanding,* (New York: Bobbs-Merrill, 1955), section 5.

14. Immanuel Kant, *The Critique of Practical Reason,* (New York: Bobbs-Merrill (1783) (1950), Book 2, chapter 2, section 5.

15. See N.L. Geisler and Win Corduan, *Philosophy of Religion,* (Grand Rapids, Michigan: Baker Book House, 1988), chapter 6.

16. See C.S. Lewis, *Mere Christianity,* (New York: The Macmillan Company, 1943), Book 1.

17. Ibid., pp. 45-46.

18. Augustine, *On the Predestination of the Saints,* in Philip Schaff ed. *Nicene and Post-Nicene Fathers* (Grand Rapids, Michigan: Eerdmans, 1979), p. 5.

19. Peter Kreeft, *Between Heaven and Hell,* (Downers Grove, Illinois: InterVarsity Press, 1982), p. 16.

Chapter Six
Science and Creation

1. Alfred North Whitehead, *Science and the Modern World,* (New York: The Free Press, 1925), p. 13.

2. M.B. Foster, "The Christian Doctrine of Creation" in *Mind* (1934), p. 448.

3. Francis Bacon, *Novum Organum and Related Writings,* Fulton H. Andersen ed. (New York: Bobbs-Merrill, 1960), 1.129.119.

4. Sir Isaac Newton, "General Scholium" in *Mathematical Principles of Natural Philosophy*, (1687) in *Great Books of the Western World*, Robert M. Hutchins ed. (Chicago: Encyclopedia Britannica, n.d.), p. 369.
5. See Norman L. Geisler and Kerby Anderson, *Origin Science*, (Grand Rapids, Michigan: Baker Book House, 1987), chapter 2.
6. Ibid., chapter 3-4.
7. Ibid., chapter 6.
8. Ibid., pp. 131-132.
9. Francis Bacon, ibid., 2.2.121.
10. David Hume, *The Letters of David Hume*, J.Y.Y. Greig ed. 2 vols. (Oxford: Clarendon, 1932), 1.187.
11. See N.L. Geisler, ibid., pp. 130-131.
12. See David Hume, *Enquiry Concerning Human Understanding*, (New York: Bobbs-Merrill, 1950), sect. 5.
13. See Geisler, ibid., pp. 137-147.
14. Robert Jastrow, *God and the Astronomers* (New York: Norton, 1978), p. 111.
15. Ibid., p. 95.
16. Ibid., p. 114.
17. Robert Jastrow, *Until the Sun Dies* (New York: Norton, 1977), p. 62.
18. This section follows the excellent book by Charles Thaxton, et. al., *The Mystery of Life's Origin* (New York: Philosophical Library, 1984).
19. Leslie Orgel, *The Origins of Life* (New York: Wiley, 1973), p. 189.
20. Michael Polanyi, "Life's Irreducible Structure" in *Science*, (1968) 160.1308.
21. Herbert Yockey, "Self Organization Origin of Life Scenarios and Information Theory" in *Journal of Theoretical Biology* (1981), p. 16.
22. Carl Sagan, *Broca's Brain* (New York: Random House, 1980), p. 275.
23. Allan Sandage, "A Scientist Reflects on Religious Belief" in *Truth: An Interdisciplinary Journal of Christian Thought* (1985) 1.54.
24. Louis Agassiz, *American Journal of Science* (1860).
25. Theodosius Dobzhansky, *The Origins of Prebiological Systems and Their Molecular Matrices*, S.W. Fox ed. (New York: Academic, 1965), p. 310.
26. Robert Jastrow, from an interview in *Christianity Today* (Aug. 6, 1982), p. 17. See also Frank Tipler and John Barrow, *The Anthropic Cosmological Principle* (Oxford: Clarendon Press, 1986).
27. There are four main views on origins: 1) Theistic Creation, 2) Theistic Evolution, 3) Naturalistic Creation, and 4) Naturalistic Evolution (see Geisler, ibid., Appendix 2).
28. For a current critique of this view see Michael Denton, *Evolution: A Theory in Crisis* (Bethesda, Maryland: Adler & Adler Publisher, 1986).
29. Augustine, *City of God* in Schaff, ibid., vol. 2, 11.6.
30. Ibid., 14.11.
31. Ibid., 11.2
32. Aquinas, *Summa Theologica* in Pegis ibid., 1.72.1.
33. Pius XII, *Humani Generis*. In the 1950 encyclical *Humani Generis*, Pope

Pius XII reaffirms this teaching:

> The Magisterium of the Church has nothing against the doctrine of evolution, inasmuch as it seeks the origin of the human body in a pre-existing and living matter—for the Catholic faith commands us to believe that the souls have been created directly by God—but in such a way that it is subject to research and discussion by experts . . .

34. Clifford Wilson, *The Language Gap*, (Grand Rapids, Michigan: Zondervan Publishing Co., 1984), pp. 147-153.
35. Quoted ibid., p. 153, emphasis added.
36. Ibid., p. 154.
37. Sagan, *Cosmos* (New York: Random House, 1980), p. 278.
38. See Geisler, ibid., p. 149.
39. L. Harrison Matthew, "Introduction" to Darwin's *On the Origin of Species*, (London: Dent, 1971), p. xi.
40. Carl Sagan, *Broca's Brain* (New York: Random House, 1979), p. 11.
41. Sagan, *Cosmos*, ibid., p. xiii.
42. Charles Darwin, *Letter to Lyell*, Oct. 20, 1859.
43. Alfred Wallace, *The World of Life* (1910) as quoted in *The Encyclopedia of Philosophy*, Paul Edwards ed. (New York: The Macmillan Company & The Free Press, 1967) 8.276.

Chapter Seven
Respect for the Creation

1. Carl Sagan, *Cosmos* (New York: Random House, 1980), 4.
2. Ibid., p. 33.
3. Ibid., p. 345.
4. Ibid., p. 4.
5. Carl Sagan, *UFO's—A Scientific Debate* (Ithaca, New York: Cornell University press, 1972), p. xv.
6. Sagan, *Broca's Brain* (New York: Random House, 1979), p. 58.
7. Sagan, *Cosmos*, ibid., p. 5.
8. Sagan, *Broca's Brain*, ibid., p. 275.
9. Friedrich Nietzsche, *Gay Science* in Walter Kaufmann, *The Portable Nietzsche* (New York: The Viking Press, 1968), p. 95.
10. Ibid., p. 96.
11. Nietzsche, *Thus Spoke Zarathustra* in Walter Kaufmann, ibid., p. 125.
12. Jean Paul Sartre, *The Flies* in Sartre, *No Exit and Three Other Plays* (New York: Vintage Books, 1946), pp. 121-123.
13. Jean Paul Sartre, *Being and Nothingness* (New York: Philosophical Library, 1956), p. 766.
14. Paul Kurtz, *Humanist Manifestos I & II* (Buffalo, New York: Prometheus Press, 1973), p. 8.
15. Ibid.

16. Ibid.
17. Ibid., p. 16.
18. Ibid., p. 17.
19. Ibid., p. 18.
20. Ibid., p. 19.
21. See J.I. Packer and T. Howard, *Christianity: The True Humanism* (Waco, Texas: Word Books, 1985) and Norman L. Geisler, *Is Man the Measure: An Evaluation of Contemporary Humanism* (Grand Rapids, Michigan: Baker Book House, 1983), chapter 8.
22. Thomas Aquinas, *Summa Theologica* in Pegis, *Basic Writings of Aquinas* (New York: Random House, 1944), 1.93.9.
23. See Lorin Wilkinson, *Earthkeeping: Christian Stewardship of Natural Resources* (Grand Rapids, Michigan: Eerdmans, 1980), p. 256.
24. C.S. Lewis, *The Abolition of Man* (New York: Macmillan, 1947), p. 69.
25. Marion A. Habig, ed., *St. Francis of Assisi: Writings and Early Biographies* (Chicago: Franciscan Herald Press, 1975), pp. 130-131.
26. Adolf Hitler, *Mein Kamph* (London: Hurst and Blackett Ltd., 1939), p. 242.
27. Ibid., p. 88.
28. William Brennen, *Abortion Holocaust: Today's Final Solution* (St. Louis: Landmark Press, 1983), p. 62.
29. Peter Singer, *Practical Ethics* (New York: Cambridge University Press, 1979) pp. 122-123.

Chapter Eight
Reverence for the Creator

1. Friedrich Scheiermacher, *On Religion: Speeches to Its Cultural Despisers,* trans, by J. Oman (New York: Frederick Unger Publishing Co., 1955), p. 39.
2. Sigmund Freud, *The Future of an Illusion* (Garden City, New York: Anchor Books, Doubleday & Company, Inc., 1964), p. 52.
3. Julian Huxley, *Religion Without Revelation* (New York: Mentor, 1957), p. 77.
4. Charles Darwin, *Letter to Lyell,* Oct. 20, 1859.
5. Charles Darwin, "Introduction" to *On the Origin of Species,* 3rd ed. See American Library edition, New York, 1958.
6. Cited by James Moore in the *Post-Darwinian Controversies,* (New York: Cambridge University Press, 1979), p. 230.
7. Ernst Haeckel, *The Riddle of the Universe* (New York: Harper & Brothers Publishers, 1900), p. 337.
8. Ibid.
9. Carl Sagan, *Cosmos* (New York: Random House, 1980), p. 345.
10. Ibid., p. 52.
11. Ibid., p. 27.
12. Ibid., p. 282.

13. Ibid., p. 5.
14. Carl Sagan, *Broca's Brain* (New York: Random House, 1979), p. 287.
15. Ibid., p. 290.
16. Sagan, *Cosmos,* ibid., p. 33.
17. Sagan, *Broca's Brain,* ibid., p. 291.
18. Sagan, *Cosmos,* ibid., p. 243.
19. Harry Binswanger, in a taped debate April 9, 1984 at the University of Florida. Available from Quest Tapes: P.O. Box 4648, Lynchburg, Virginia, 24502.
20. Albert Camus, *The Rebel* (New York: Alfred A. Knopf, Vintage Books, 1956), p. 147.
21. Jean Paul Sartre, *Words* (New York: George Braziller, 1964), p. 102.
22. Frederich Nietzsche, Letter to Overbeck (July 2, 1885) in Walter Kaufmann, *The Portable Nietzsche* (New York: The Viking Press, 1968), p. 441.
23. Paul Kurtz, *Humanist Manifestos I & II* (Buffalo: Prometheus Books, 1973), p. 8.
24. David Ehrenfeld, *The Arrogance of Humanism* (New York: Oxford University Press, 1978), p. 3.
25. John Calvin, *Institutes of the Christian Religion* (Grand Rapids, Michigan: Eerdmans, 1957) 1.105.
26. J.I. Packer, *Knowing God* (Downers Grove, Illinois: InterVarsity Press, 1973), p. 183.
27. C.S. Lewis, *Reflections on the Psalms* (New York: Hartcourt, Brace and Company, 1958), p. 92.
28. Ibid.

Other Books of Interest in the Knowing the Truth Series

Knowing the Truth of God's Love
Peter Kreeft

With unusual clarity, Peter Kreeft points out that the man or woman who begins to glimpse the God who is Creator, Redeemer, and Lover of our souls, will never be the same. He describes Scripture as a love story and then tells why divine love answers our deepest problems. Posing the hard questions about love that rankle the heart, Peter Kreeft never settles for easy answers. Instead, he exposes today's superficial attitudes about love in order to lead people to a deeper understanding of what it means to be loved by God. *$8.95*

Knowing the Truth about Heaven and Hell
Harry Blamires

Harry Blamires believes that many people are in danger of forgetting the truth about heaven and hell, to their peril. He points out that our choices have an immense impact upon our eternal well-being—unending happiness with God or the unimaginable sorrow of eternal anguish. *Knowing the Truth about Heaven and Hell* will bring you into touch with ultimate realities and lead you to a deeper understanding of the Father's desire to unite all men and women to himself forever. The invitation is clear. The choice is ours. *$8.95*

Knowing the Truth about the Resurrection
William L. Craig

Are the accounts in the Gospels of Jesus' burial, the empty tomb, and his resurrection appearances reliable? Or are they biased? Did the disciples really see the risen Jesus? Laying out the arguments, both pro and con, William L. Craig presents a compelling case for the resurrection as an event of earth-shattering significance for the human race. If Jesus really rose and now lives, we can have a relationship with him that anticipates our own resurrection on the Last Day. Here is a convincing and compelling look at the resurrection for Christians and skeptics alike. *$8.95*

Available at your Christian bookstore or from:
**Servant Publications • Dept. 209 • P.O. Box 7455
Ann Arbor, Michigan 48107**
Please include payment plus $1.00 per book
for postage and handling.
*Send for our FREE catalog of Christian
books, music, and cassettes.*